Michael Kerrigan

A 21st CENTURY CLASSIC!
You Have All the Choices There Are. Learn How to Make...

THE BEST ONES!

What Choice Do I Have?

★ ★ ★

26 Choice Secrets to Help You Achieve the Results You Want in All Areas of Life and Work

★ ★ ★

Foreword by John Fuhrman, Author of
Reject Me—I Love It!
The World's Number One Process for Handling Rejection

What Choice Do I Have?

Copyright © 2002 Michael Kerrigan
Michael@SeventhRail.com
www.SeventhRail.com
ISBN 0-938716-29-8

Published by
Possibility Press
posspress@aol.com
www.possibilitypress.com

Manufactured in the United States of America

Dedication

This book is dedicated to my father, for his
encouragement and to my mother, for her optimism.

Contents

Foreword

A Choice to Follow Your Dreams

*"Destiny is not a matter of chance,
it is a matter of choice.
It is not a thing to be waited for;
it is a thing to be achieved."*
William Jennings Bryan

What an honor! I am excited to tell you why this book is going to become an important part of your life. The privilege of being asked to write the foreword of any book is the highest of peer recognition. The honor I feel for being selected to foreword such an important book cannot be put into words.

My only hope is to create the sense of urgency inside you to read and apply this life-enhancing information. Do that and the world will become a better place for you as well as others—*because of your choices.* And the coming pages will compel you to take action. You will no longer allow yourself to be a victim of circumstances. Instead, you will more actively choose to create your own.

Choice. What a powerful concept. It's what separates us from every living organism on the planet. Consciously or unconsciously, we *choose* our life path or allow others to do so, which is also a choice. Unfortunately, many people don't understand that they themselves made practically all the choices which have lead to their current circumstances. Michael Kerrigan's excellent work will clear up any doubt you may have had

vi WHAT CHOICE DO I HAVE?—*Michael Kerrigan*

about that. It will also encourage you to take back any control of your life that you have let go—*by teaching you how to make better choices.*

Do you believe the world is split between the *haves* and *have nots*? Do you believe there are those who were born to make it and those who were born to work for those who make it? Unfortunately, many people drive themselves to an early grave resenting the people they believe were just "lucky" in life.

Fortunately, the "have/have not" theory is totally incorrect. The world is, in fact, divided into two groups. But they're not the groups many were led to believe existed. This book shares how you can identify them and decide which group *you'd* like to belong to. It also provides the guidance you'll need to become part of the group you choose, and more importantly, how to share that information with others.

My perspective is that the two groups are the *haves* and the *have tos*. First, there are those who *have* already made the choice and are now reaping the rewards. Then there are those who *have to*—they choose to let others choose for them. In either case, the choices made or not made will certainly determine where they spend the rest of their lives.

Your life and where you are right now is the sum total of every choice you've ever made or allowed others to make for you. Those of you not satisfied with your current station in life may argue that you wouldn't *choose* to be where you are in a million years. While that may well be true, the fact of the matter is every choice has a consequence and you are now living the consequences of your past choices!

It's a lot like complaining about never winning the lottery, yet every week *choosing* not to buy a ticket. I believe if you ask most people if they'd love to win the lottery, they'd say yes. So, while you may want the rewards that come with the winning numbers, if you choose not to ever take a chance on a ticket, you can never win. It's as simple as that.

Did you know that the average writer quits after being turned down by ten publishers? Over 100 publishers had rejected me before I signed a contract for my first book, *Reject Me – I Love it! 21 Secrets for Turning Rejection Into Direction.* It is my belief that many other writers *choose* to let the opinions of a few determine their lives. I *chose* to do whatever it took to see my name on the cover of a book.

The result of so many writers quitting the race to be published is that you'll never read what could have been a great help to you. No one will ever be inspired by their potential to help others because they didn't persist. And many of those same would-be authors will tell anyone who listens that getting published is simply a matter of "luck" and who you know. But simply because I *chose* to continue the race, I have been able to help over one million people—a result that a few short years ago was just a dream!

Simply because I made a choice, I'm now doing what I choose to do while the wanna-be authors who gave up aren't authors. They simply *chose* to give up! Have I spoken all over the world because I'm more talented? Hardly. Do I have an inside track to the publishing and speaking industry? No. Am I just lucky? Not even close.

The simple truth is I was willing to do what each of you is about to discover in this great book. I was willing to ask myself, "What choice do I have?" I then made the choice to commit myself to writing and going through the noes until a publisher said yes to a book proposal and an organization said yes to my speaking for them.

Now I can honestly say that I am living the life of my dreams. But the only question is, "How about you?" Just ask yourself, "What Choice Do I Have?" To go from where you are today to where you want to be tomorrow is simply a matter of choice—not chance. After all, you have all the choices there are!

I wish you much success in choosing what's best for your future. *What Choice Do I Have?* can help you do that. Read it and start making better choices.

John Fuhrman
Frame of Mind, Inc.
Manchester, New Hampshire

Introduction

What Are the Best Choices for You?

*"Any hope of achieving your dreams
is virtually impossible if you're holding back and choosing to settle
for things as you may have done in the past."*
Michael Kerrigan

We all want what's best for us and those we care about, right? At least we're *supposed* to. But, all too often there's a gap—our choices and actions don't always support our wants!

When a significant event finally *does* occur, oftentimes initiated by someone else whose choices and actions support *their* wants, we may be forced to move on or make a choice that may affect the rest of our lives. At this pivotal point, many of us can actually *see* our potential and how we could pursue our dreams. So why don't we always embrace it? Because in all too many cases, we panic out of fear of change, and actually run away from our dreams!

"Thank goodness I'm past that," we may sigh with relief. And then we return to whatever we were doing before—we've avoided the risk of change but never set ourselves up to experience what our life *could* have been like.

We may discard the whole idea of reaching for something better, but our anxiety about what we *are* doing always returns. The anguish over what our lives could be like—if we had chosen to go for what we really wanted—pays us another visit.

And so it goes. We're all challenged in different areas of our lives, whether it's in relationships, our job or business, dealing with ourselves, or a myriad of other things. For example, you either have a great relationship with someone, or you don't!

Many of those in committed relationships have created happy, contented alliances. But all too many others endure this part of their lives under a cloud of second-guessing—either they know their relationship could be better, or they've settled for how it is, knowing it could be far worse.

For those without a relationship, there's the annoying daily reminder from the cartoon strip *Cathy* that they must meet the "perfect" person. There's the perception that once they're in a relationship their life will be complete. At least that's what they think until, of course, they prove themselves wrong. And underlying most of these relationship perspectives is a yearning for improvement and the desire for a life that will bring more fulfillment and happiness.

Then there's the business cycle. Those who have a job typically want a better one. And those who are without a job just want to get a foot in the door.

Another piece of the business puzzle includes millions of people who own their own businesses—many times in addition to their jobs. They have opted out of the typical job world, or are planning to do so, to take their chances on their own as storeowners, manufacturers, marketers, consultants, franchisees, direct salespeople, or in running home-based businesses.

Whether they do it voluntarily or not, all of these entrepreneurs are forced to examine their condition at least once a day: "Did I do the right thing? Why am I alone in this extra bedroom? How is it that my closest business confidante is now the cat?" Hints of doubt, pressure, indecision, and change abound—especially for those with businesses that eat up virtually all of their time.

Beyond these predictable areas of day-to-day living are the realms of change involving social relationships, health, kids, where you live, where you *don't* live, aging, politics, and even death. The list could go on indefinitely, but the message is clear: *We all need to deal with the challenges that burst into our lives, and take responsibility for the outcomes we create.* And as you may have noticed, many people don't do much of either. Their lives are like stockpiles of unresolved issues for which they blame others.

This book can help you clarify your choices and create the best outcomes possible. And who couldn't use a hand in navigating life's annoyances *and* opportunities when they appear and announce, "We're here"?

In all the areas of life just mentioned, people crave to be in charge. They'd like to have more control. People want to know the most efficient and effective way to manage the challenges they face every day.

The title of this book is what it is for a good reason. Many people either don't realize or they simply forget that their life is made up of a series of choices. In fact, you are where and what you are today because of all the choices you've made up to this point in time. And, of course, not making a choice is also a choice!

So what's the answer to the title's question? That's easy. *You have all the choices there are!* The challenges for most people in exercising them however, lies in something called the "comfort zone." It's a place where things are familiar: people, jobs, foods, attitudes, and old pairs of jeans. We like this zone because we know pretty much what to expect out of every waking moment. We rely on it to give us the things we want, or believe we want.

But the *comfort zone* most likely isn't comfortable at all, is it? Oftentimes it's just *familiar*. And it's probably a place of *stale* outcomes and *pale* rewards. It could also be called the *boring zone* or even the *settle-for zone!*

In fact, this place is really more of a *survival zone,* and it's where most people live out their lives. They're surviving, doing just enough to get by. Here they're busy, but not especially productive in terms of realizing their personal dreams.

Sadly, many people don't even realize they've lost or missed relationships and opportunities because it never occurred to them to reach out to others or experience something new. They've operated this way for as long as they can remember since *survival* doesn't require letting anyone or anything new into their lives. And in most cases, everyone around them is operating the same way, doing the same thing. They consider survival normal, and that they're doing okay.

The possibility of choosing positive change in your survival zone is almost nil. Any hope of achieving your dreams is virtually impossible when you're settled back and choosing to settle for things as you may have done in the past. Fortunately, the survival zone is nothing more than a *mental* barrier but it will keep you from making better choices—until *you* decide to take action and break through its walls.

This book will provide you with the kind of anecdotes and self-assessing exercises that will help you get your life into perspective. It will help you put together a plan to reach the goals you could never attain without choosing to go beyond the survival zone.

Without some guidance and feedback, it's all too easy to become pessimistic—to doubt our strengths and forget our basic courage—even with our best efforts to cope. Without some kind of perspective, there's a general perception that the choices we make could always be better. There's a reason that the term *buyer's remorse* is part of our language. For some reason, there's a tendency to distrust our own instincts and actions.

This book is designed to help you determine what is most important to you and to help you make the choices that will ultimately lead you to the best possible outcomes. Actively guiding yourself every day is a challenge to your courage and confidence—elements you already have, but may have simply lost touch with. But reaching for a fulfilled life—a life that is rightfully yours—is something everyone can do. Take responsibility for where you are and where you're going and you'll have the necessary control over your thoughts, dreams, and actions.

This book gives you the tools you need to make a smarter run at life. When was the last time you heard someone say, "Gee, if I only knew then what I know now"? What is covered here will enable you to do just that—harness your wisdom and experience and use it to your best advantage. You'll have the tools to direct your life in the most positive and fulfilling way you could imagine.

Regrettably, every day, millions of people run away from opportunities to improve their lives. In case after case, all over the world, people choose to stay where they are. And all too often, their choices leave them careening through life, bruised by disappointment and deflated by frustration.

But that isn't *your* choice. What separates you from so many others is your willingness to take positive action on your own behalf. And simply by picking up this book, you've done three things:

- Confirmed that you haven't yet reached your full potential.

- Shown you are willing to embrace another, more productive way of living.
- Taken positive action on your own behalf.

That willingness to be an active player in your own life is a huge step in mastering the life that awaits you. And this book can be a tremendous benefit to you in taking charge of who you are and what you *will* become. What is discussed in these pages — though addressed with modern day examples — has its roots in basic principles that reach back more than 200 years, the inseparable principles of freedom and choice.

Ever since the leaders of free countries throughout the world chose to declare their independence from opposing forces, significant challenges and opportunities have dotted their histories: the choice to ensure undying freedoms for the nations' peoples, the choice to fight wars to banish tyranny and preserve freedom, the choice to embrace people of various religious beliefs and ethnic origins. Each of these conscious acts, and countless more throughout the free world, have helped keep dreams alive by strengthening each country's foundation and helping it to endure and prosper.

Even the September 11, 2001 terrorist attack on the United States against the civilized countries of the world—calls on each of us to make a choice: to stand up and address the threat on our precious principles and hard-won freedoms, or wilt under the strain. Each of us has the capacity to empower ourselves and others, to live our lives and achieve our dreams, despite the attempts by outside forces to chip away at our confidence and challenge our will.

The day we stop dreaming and striving, terrorism wins. So now, more than ever, we need to dream big dreams and do whatever it takes to achieve them. And that is certainly the best choice of all!

How you choose to live your life will determine the legacy that will follow and the ideology that will prevail. In short, your future and your success are carried in your own two hands.

The ideas and discussions you'll find here are based, in part, on sound psychology, sociology, and other related disciplines. The message you'll discover—that of self-determination—has grown out of my experiences as a journalist, coupled with the seminars I've conducted and research I've carried out during the past decade.

Doing research and putting findings into a usable form is what I do best. I spent 11 years reporting for and editing newspapers and magazines all over the U.S. beginning in Berkeley, California and ending in Washington, D.C.

My understanding of how people cope and choose was sharpened every day I went to work. If people weren't choosing and changing—usually for the worse—they weren't a story! It was the nature of my job to watch people grapple with change and observe how they emerged from their experiences. Some, of course, fared better than others.

For example, someone always won each election. But for every winner there were two or three others who didn't assume office, being left to piece together their lives and move on. Even the winners had a whole new set of issues to deal with and tough challenges to resolve. I sometimes wondered whether they had actually won anything at all!

Then there were the businesses that closed, leaving scores of people shaking their heads at being out of work, pondering the choices they had to make. My reporting experiences also included dozens of other cases—some violent, some ironic—where people's lives changed instantly and dramatically, forever. And my experience as a mediator has given me a clear understanding of people's motives when their wants, needs, and desires are challenged.

You'll have plenty of opportunities to put these anecdotes and ideas to good use. Remember that taking that first step toward a new goal or a new way of living is something you can do anytime. There's no age restriction or income requirement. The only things necessary are your will to act and your desire to give yourself the life you truly want—by making the best choices you can. My hope is that you find this book helpful in doing so.

"**D**estiny is not a matter of chance, it is a matter of choice. It is not a thing to be waited for; it is a thing to be achieved."

—William Jennings Bryan

Chapter 1

What Do You Want?
The Most Meaningful Choice You Can Make

*"When you opt for your dreams,
you open yourself up to a whole
new world of possibilities. You'll grow
and learn in ways you probably
never have imagined."*
Michael Kerrigan

The quality of your life depends on making important, meaningful choices. And there's one choice that serves as the foundation for defining who you are and where you are going. It's the fundamental choice that drives all others, and results in making your life and its opportunities work *for* you.

Address that choice honestly and you'll be well on your way to making a chain of positive choices. This ripple of truth will help you manage difficult issues and identify your true calling.

Of course, you can always choose another road—you can opt to be less than honest with yourself. But if you do, you're destined to stay right where you are. You'll get lost in a swirl of people and their agendas that grow and evolve without much concern for you and your desires. The key question you need to ask yourself is: *"What do I want?"*

We're all confronted by this question many times a day. It begins the moment that wonderful alarm clock blasts through the silence of the early morning darkness. Would you like to sleep in, or do you really *want* to get out of bed and go to work?

The question continues to persist during your morning commute. Do you want to give someone else a ride in the carpool you may be in, or do you want to review the details of a presentation you need to make later in the day? Do you want to listen to the radio, an educational/motivational tape or CD, or ride in silence?

What do you want?

Sometimes the answer is subconscious, nothing more than a reflex. Yes, no. Do, don't. File, throw away. At other times, the answer is calculated to avoid confrontations, win compliments, or simply buy time. And sometimes it's even "I don't know!"

Consider Lynn's answer to that daunting question. It was always complex. She wanted to avoid confrontation, because it meant fighting. She thought clashing viewpoints could never be resolved through discussion. She believed such exchanges always flared into arguments, and she really disliked it when people argued.

Lynn also wanted to buy time. More time meant not having to meet deadlines and less pressure. Pressure made her nervous, and "I'm already frail," Lynn told herself. She was able to survive this way for seven years. She avoided uncomfortable conversations and those dreaded deadlines right up to the day she was fired. What Lynn wanted may have been comfortable for her, but it was unrealistic for everyone else. Her wants were impractical and she wasn't being honest with herself. Lynn's behavior highlights one of the critical elements in dealing with change, and that is *honesty*.

When you're honest with yourself, the choices you make are more likely to get you what you want. Honest answers will usher you to the destination you want to reach. Without honesty, each choice you make is built on a lie—the father of disappointment.

For Lynn, the disappointment was being fired. Honesty about how she was spending her time, her level of commitment, and her relationships with others in her office could have saved her job. Unfortunately, she chose deception.

So, *what do you want?*

Do you want to put in another hour of work to complete that special project before you leave the office? Or would you like to finish reading that book before you go to bed? The questions demanding answers don't end until you turn out the light and drift off to sleep. And sometimes they don't even stop then.

The questions are pervasive, and typically involve minor issues—what to have for lunch, whether or not to exercise, which television show to watch, or whether to watch TV at all! Occasionally, you're asked to make choices that can have profound impacts, not only for you but also for your family, co-workers, business associates, and any employees you may have. Now ask yourself these four questions:

- Is this profession right for me?
- Do I want to invest more time and energy in working my job?
- Do I want my own business?
- Do I want to stay in this relationship, or any relationship?

Handing Off Responsibility

Before you answer any of these questions, it's important to understand what brought you to this point in your life. The reasons you are where you are today are based on a host of choices that were made throughout your life. Initially, they were choices that were made *for* you—usually by your parents.

As a child, what *you* thought probably made little difference. You felt as though you were just along for the ride and certainly not "in charge." The choices made for and about you involved the belief systems of those who were guiding you—that education is or isn't important, that hard work is or isn't the key to a better life, and that treating people fairly is or isn't a guiding principle in establishing meaningful relationships.

In addition, choices of religion were made for you. You may have been raised as a strong Catholic, observing Mass each Sunday and following the direction of the Pope. Or you may have been raised as an Orthodox Jew, with strict adherence to Yom Kippur, the Day of Atonement. Or you may have been raised with another religion or no religious affiliation at all.

Choices were also made for you about where you were raised. And directly linked to geography were cultural biases that influenced you—the sports you played, the books you read, and the people you called friends.

But at some point in your life that all started to change. Your parents began making fewer choices *for* you. You began to decide what clothes to wear and what food to eat. You chose where to go to school and the nature of your work. And you decided what relationships to establish and how to live your life.

Where you are today is the sum total of all those choices—the good, the bad, and, yes, the *ugly*. And just as those past choices got you where you are today, the choices you make from now on will determine where you go tomorrow. Just make sure to choose what *you* want. And above all, make sure you're honest with yourself when you do.

Your Survival or Your Dreams?

When it comes to choosing your goals and the paths to reach them, there are basically two ways to go. You can settle for *survival*, or you can pursue your *dreams*.

When you opt for your dreams, you open yourself up to a whole new world of possibilities. You'll grow and learn in ways you could never have imagined. And while most of those adventures will be positive, others won't. Not every step toward your dreams will be easy or magical. But each step will be based on possibilities and potential.

You'll need to make conscious decisions and ongoing choices that won't always be welcomed by others. In fact, some of those people and circumstances will need to be left behind—and that could be challenging. After all, who wants to abandon the people and things they've spent so much time with? But if those relationships aren't supporting you in achieving the life you want and need, can you really justify keeping them?

Are you still friends with classmates from first grade, high school, or college? If you go through life with more than a couple of true friends, you are fortunate indeed. It's just a fact of life. As we grow and become who we were created to be, relationships change. There simply isn't enough time to be close to everyone you've ever known and accomplish new goals in your life.

This doesn't mean you discard people along the way either. The relationships that are precious to you will remain so. It's just that, as you move on, new people will come into your life and occupy some of your time. Who knows? You may have yet to meet the person who will be your best friend for life!

True friends will remain so even if you don't see them as much as you used to. And if they choose not to participate in whatever changes you choose to make in your life, they will always support you and your new positive choices. If they don't, they're probably not your friends!

Adjusting to new people and changing situations doesn't happen overnight, but it can be made much easier by:

- Understanding where you're comfortable in your life and why.
- Identifying how the relationships you currently have are either helping you or hindering you.

Proactively choosing what you want will reward you with personal growth and virtually unlimited opportunities. You'll be moving in a direction that will help you realize your dreams.

Of course, there is always a second option when you are navigating change: It's called *survival*. But choosing the familiar is not likely to take you on the path to your dreams. And it probably won't be very exciting or rewarding either.

In most cases, pursuing the familiar keeps you exactly where you are. It leaves you walking in circles, covering the same territory with the scenery never changing. And sadly, this often leads to a life lived on little more than a treadmill.

We all operate in a zone where we mix with familiar people and places, habits and beliefs. Yes, staying in it can give you a sense of stability and the belief that things are normal. But your experience here will be essentially what it's always been—going to the same places, engaging in the same conversations and performing the same rituals. And that's the best you can hope for.

Now for some people this may be fine. There is a lot to be said for stability. For many people, though, it's hard to separate stability from drudgery. And since you're reading this book, it's obvious you're ready to make some changes. Guiding yourself toward your goals and dreams requires making new choices. And analyzing them and selecting what's best for you takes some thought.

You Have All the Choices There Are!

You now have the chance to choose exactly what you want. You'll find a list of options, from generating enough income to live out your wildest dreams to spending unlimited time with your family, or for learning or travel. Take a look at the list. Your dream may be on it, or your idea of true happiness and success may be something no one has ever thought of before. No matter what, though, examine the list and then identify what it is you want more than anything else in the world. Here are some ideas for you:

- More time with your family.
- Enough time and money to live out your wildest dreams.
- Social status.
- A leadership role in the community.
- A beautiful new home.
- An outlet for your creative energy.
- Worthwhile, satisfying relationships.
- A more meaningful career or a business of your own.
- Unlimited time for thought and study.
- Opportunities to travel.

Next, you'll find some questions relating to your desires. They'll help you focus on how you're going to achieve your dream. You may have some answers now or need to invest some additional time charting your course. Either way, be sure to answer them. They will help you clarify what you really want and how you're going to go about getting it:

- First, is your want now within your reach?
- If it's not within your reach, how are you going to get it?
- Do you have the right education?
- Do you need financing?
- Do you need to adjust your family or other obligations?
- Are you in the right place—geographically—to get what it is you want?
- Who can help you, and what can they do to assist you?

Answering these questions honestly will give you a better sense of what you want to pursue, as well as the challenges you may encounter along the way. Answering them now will help put your goal into perspective, giving you a clearer picture of how you're going to achieve it. This is an essential first step in bringing positive, productive change into your life. Identifying what you *really* want and plotting your course to achieve it makes for an exciting, challenging adventure—one that you've custom made for yourself.

Chapter 2

Break Away from the Crowd
Find Your True Potential

*"What's important is moving beyond that predictable,
marginal behavior—whatever your age. Reaching your
potential is really what life is all about."*
Michael Kerrigan

In the third grade, after three intense months of transitioning from printing to writing, I was shocked when I read my report card. Under the heading, *Comments*, in the steady hand of Sister Christopher, was a brief assessment of what she believed I was really all about. "Michael," she wrote, "is not living up to his potential."

Now I'd been able to interpret the letter grades given to me since the first grade: A, B, C, and so on. And now the rest of the report began to make sense, where before it was just so much decoration. And I didn't like what I read.

Nuns aren't supposed to say things like that, I thought. They were to be nice. Of course, I knew better. They were *supposed* to teach. But in reading the remark, as neatly and clearly as it was written, I was still angry. And now that I'm old enough to look back on the way I was performing, it makes absolute sense. I *had* joined the ranks of the average.

I fit in, perfectly, because I didn't feel the need to stand out. At an early age, I had already gotten lazy, doing just enough to get by. Reluctantly, I'd raise my hand to answer a question, but only occasionally. My potential was something I didn't spend much time pursuing. I was more interested in Jeff climbing around on his desk, and the notes flying back and forth between Julie and Marcie. My thoughts drifted to soccer, the candy store, and what was on television.

Sister Christopher was right. I wasn't living up to my potential. The important things—studying and performing—were secondary to me, at best.

You may have been in the same position yourself. Or you may be there now. Many of us don't bother to leave our childhood habits behind once we become adults. Sure, we usually learn to read and write, balance a checkbook, operate a computer, and get a job. And all that's necessary to live, but it's nothing more than average.

What's important is moving beyond that predictable, marginal behavior—whatever your age may be. After all, reaching your potential is really what life is all about. Have you made the *choice* to be more than average? Are you living up to your potential? Or are you, like most people, only 10 percent of what you could be?

Just Looking Out the Window

Your diversions may be more interesting and fun than what you do for a living, and they probably beckon you all the time. These attention-grabbers take the form of television, computer or video games, hunting, sports, hobbies, travel, poker, golf, aerobics, and every other activity under the sun. While these things are generally harmless, they can become obsessions. But activities done for instant gratification can keep you from achieving the goals that are truly important to you. They can keep you from being nothing more than average.

Now let's examine the balance between your ambition and your effort by honestly answering two simple questions:

- First: What is really important to you? What do you feel passionately about, i.e., your family, financial freedom, your religion, or maybe even your golf game?
- Second: How are you spending your time?

For instance, you may dream of being financially free or climbing a mountain, but have you started working on it? Your answer to the second question is meant to lend some perspective to the response you gave to the first. If you're giving a lot of time to activities that don't relate to what's important to you, ask yourself, "Why?"

Remember, how you use your time is your choice. And it's up to you to *invest* it in the most productive way you can. Why not invest it in your goals and dreams?

All too often, however, many people surrender their right to perform at their highest levels. They give their best efforts to bosses and acquaintances, the whims of kids, and those who don't have their best interests at heart. Many people surrender what is rightfully theirs to an array of people, some of them perfect strangers! But surrender can also be made to things—those possessions and activities that get in the way of your dreams.

Surrender also comes in the way you behave, or if you fail to say exactly what you mean. It comes when you're given a choice but, instead of exercising your options, you let someone else make that choice for you. Surrender comes when you choose the apparently easiest course, rather than the one that will serve you best.

The failure to pursue dreams, and simply go with the flow, helps keep people average. Unfortunately, the announcement that tells adults to give their greatest effort isn't as dramatic as it is for most elementary school kids. We aren't shaken by a note to our parents. We aren't "tied" to our desks for fidgeting, as Jeff was. We aren't sent to the principal's office for passing notes, as Julie and Marcie were. Our job performance reports may be fair or sufficient—nothing above average—which means we'll basically stay stuck in a rut.

In relationships, you can easily slip into negative behaviors without a second thought. They create a frame of mind where dreams are ignored or completely forgotten. And if you get a wakeup call to *change your behavior,* it may arrive in the form of a firing or divorce!

In other areas of your life, the quest for growth and knowledge may slow down and die without even a nod to its passing. It's as if those one-time dreams never existed. And that becomes the norm. So where's the reward?

- Rewards are found in truthfully making choices based on what you really want.
- Rewards come in knowing what's going on around you and not being caught by surprise.
- Rewards are found in delaying gratification and not giving in to diversions—so you can live up to your potential.

Elementary school was a long time ago, and it's time to let go of the average mindset that may have since developed. It's time to re-focus by choosing who you really are and striving for your dream, and by being true to what you believe in and desire. Only then can you reach your true potential and claim the life you dream of, but may have never dared to pursue.

Chapter 3

Blaze Your Own Trail
It's Never Too Late to Change

*"You can look back at where you've been
with a sense of regret and lost opportunity.
Or you can turn your experiences into a life-
fulfilling adventure that will be
the stuff of family legends."*
Michael Kerrigan

At one time or another, we've all found ourselves in the middle of a really awkward situation.

You're at a large family holiday dinner. Your Aunt Bunny puts down her now-empty cup of coffee on the white starched table cloth, leans back in her chair, and gets a far away look in her eyes. After an uncomfortable silence, when you're not sure if she's nodded off with her eyes open or just suffered a stroke, she utters something like: "If I hadn't married your Uncle Arthur, my life would have been much, much happier. What on earth did I see in that man?"

Okay, this is only an example. And we've just gone through the easy part—the uncomfortable, disappointing life of *somebody else*.

So what about you? Are you dreading the time when you play the role of Bunny in the family Christmas drama? Won't it be great when you can lean back in *your* chair and depress the spirit out of everyone by reminiscing about a life gone wrong?

There is a whole range of perspectives you can carry through life. Will you look back at where you've been with a sense of regret and lost opportunity? Or will you turn your life experiences into fulfilling adventures that will be the stuff that makes for family legends?

When analyzing their lives, far too many people say, "Gee, if only I had done this or that" and they assume the role of Bunny. Then, one Christmas, they suddenly find themselves reminiscing around the dinner table and complaining about life—so far—as a waste of time.

The great news is it's *never* too late to change. And it's important to realize that your past does not determine your future—unless you let it! Unfortunately, as many people age, their willingness to go out and do new things and experience new people fades—but you don't have to be one of them!

Now with Bunny in mind, focus on your own situation: How could *your* life have been different? What other roads could you have taken? When you can envision a different road through life, take one more step and answer these two questions:

- Where would you be now if you had taken that road?
- What would your life be like now if you had entered into that *other* relationship, taken that *other* job, moved to *another* state, or seized a new opportunity?

Obviously you can't know for sure, but give these questions your best, educated guess.

Now, of course, your life may be great—you may not have wanted to live it any other way. If that's the case, congratulations. Stay the course. But for many people—especially those who want to reach for more success, opportunities, and fulfillment in their lives—remaining on the same path would be fruitless. It will only lead to more frustration and pain.

Hopefully, the above will help you get more comfortable in making clear, positive choices. You've seen how the process works and pictured what the outcomes can be. So if you don't like where you are in some area of your life, make the choice to change it.

And start doing it now!

Chapter 4

Take Charge of Your Life
Set Your Sights on a New Beginning

"Moving forward is a process,
not a single, simple encounter."
Michael Kerrigan

In an ideal world, we'd all have total control of our lives. Each of us would make clear goal-oriented decisions. We'd choose where to live and work, who would be in and out of our lives, how our schedules would mesh, how much money we'd make, how we would use our time, and how the details of our day would click.

As much as we may wish for it, an ideal world is challenging to come by. That's not to say achieving it isn't possible. We just need to know how to go about making it a reality.

Think of one issue or relationship that you're allowing to control you, rather than you controlling it. This can apply to just about anything—a partner, a job, a possession, or something else. The reason for a situation like this even developing is, frankly, quite simple. Most of us don't know where changing a relationship or a behavior will lead. Our fear of ending up with something or someone worse seems to be too much to deal with. So we refuse to take the initiative, and let well enough alone.

In all too many cases we rationalize what we have, devise a strategy to deal with it, and settle for where we are. And there we stay. The idea of exerting control, leading to positive outcomes, is forgotten. But the consequences of this approach to life are disappointing, at best. It leaves millions of people feeling trapped. It's like breathing with one lung. You can never get enough air to really accelerate, so you never become vigorously involved in anything.

But regaining control of your life becomes very real when you thoughtfully *choose* to initiate change. It also requires that you get past that first glance at a better way of living that tells you it's too complex or threatening to deal with, much less achieve. Moving forward is a process, not a single, simple encounter. And to sustain it you need to follow your dream.

Accentuate the Positive

Psychologist Erich Fromm wrote about two kinds of change—positive and negative. Negative change, he said, was running away from something, be it a person, place, situation, or thing. And change for the sake of change—evolution without a goal—leads nowhere. At the same time, Fromm characterized positive change as moving *toward* something—people, places, situations, or rewards.

Goal setting plays an instrumental role in achieving success. Later we'll look at the steps involved and allowing a new outlook to work for you. But start choosing your goals now. It's never too early to begin identifying your dream and where you ultimately want to be.

Start to Tinker

Think of one situation, relationship, or event that you're allowing to control you because you don't know where changing it could lead.

First, think of what's likely to happen if you start tinkering with the relationship. *Chaos* might be the first thing that pops into your mind, and it's typically experienced when we're introduced to a new situation. Fortunately, chaos doesn't last. It can't. Even in the most complex environments, people not only survive, but they can also learn from it and move on.

Second, identify where you're going to land once you take the leap from your old environment. What are your possibilities? Think beyond the mental barriers you have that are now limiting you in some way—any way. Allow yourself to consider new ways of behaving. Once you start thinking creatively, new options will present themselves. And the situations that now look like traps will become nothing more than memories of the way things *were*—something you grew through and beyond.

Chapter 5

Escape the *Survival* Trap
Step Beyond Your Familiar Zone

*"Stepping beyond your survival zone will
give you a life that offers the prospect for the
greatest opportunities and the richest rewards.
Why? Because it's outside your survival zone
that your dreams reside."*
Michael Kerrigan

In early March 1992, I boarded a stair-climber exercise machine and started pumping my way through another hurried workout. A man in his mid-40s got on the machine next to mine and began his own routine. Soon, we were locked in conversation.

He introduced himself as Tex and told me a bit about himself. He then listened as I took my turn, briefly telling him about my career as a journalist and how I now helped people manage challenges and reach their goals.

He thought about what I had said, and then suggested that he didn't think making choices and changing direction was all that difficult. Tex shared that he had recently chosen to change his profession after a 15-year career as a contractor and builder.

Naturally, this transition opened a new chapter for him and his family. They needed to manage their smaller income differently, and make some other sacrifices as they were getting their new business off the ground. And now he was—a llama rancher. And that was that, Tex concluded.

Then I began to have my doubts. Perhaps I had misread the whole issue. Maybe choosing and forging ahead in a new direction wasn't the jarring, sometimes frightening experience my research said it was.

But something seemed wrong with this picture. Tex seemed too casual about this life-reversing move. He seemed too calm and controlled about giving up what he'd done for so long, especially since he was now doing something so foreign. After all, a llama isn't even a cow, much less a piece of lumber.

"And how long had you been thinking about making this change?" I finally asked. Tex answered, "Ten years."

For ten years he had clung to a career he no longer wanted, riding out a major crash in the construction industry and a few minor recessions. For ten years he ignored what he dreamed of (being a llama rancher) in order to continue with a behavior he was familiar with—even though it definitely wasn't what he wanted.

Now a lot has been written about *comfort* zones—why they exist, who stays there, and the world outside them. But as you now may realize, the term comfort is too often substituted for what really happens in these places and that's—*survival*. And once you understand the role your survival zone plays in your making choices, the more successful you can be in your efforts to achieve goals and build new relationships.

Crowding in the Survival Zone

While everyone has a survival zone, each one is different. The survival zone serves whatever purpose you assign it, as long as what happens there is familiar.

At the heart of the survival zone are those people, places, things, and beliefs with which you are most at ease. For many people, these include family, a home, a place of worship, their full-time job or business, their favorite foods, activities with their children, a prized collection of some kind (music, dolls, memorabilia, or something else), a familiar wardrobe, and a close circle of friends. These are basically the possessions and relationships people rely on to meet their wants and needs—day after day, week after week, year in and year out.

If you encounter resistance in your survival zone, it may be your choice to shut down the challenge and get rid of it as quickly as possible. After all, what's the point in having a survival zone if the only things it offers you are challenges, or the chance that something won't go your way?

No, you don't have to do most things you don't want to in your survival zone. You don't have to change your job or business, move to a new location and home, wear different style clothes, or make new friends. You simply don't *have* to do anything differently.

The disappointing thing about survival zones, though, is that they sometimes take on lives of their own. Jobs and businesses disappear, transfers are ordered, clothes go out of style, and friends move, fall out of favor, or die. And you are left to react. Your ability to control all elements in your life, including the activities in your survival zone, does have limits. Change often happens without you choosing it, as I'm sure you've noticed.

Pull Up Your Emotional Anchors

When you're confronted with doing things differently, you can respond in one of two ways: retreat or move forward.

The first option is to retreat deeper into your survival zone in an attempt to preserve what you can of what's left. This response is triggered by anger and fear.

Anger erupts when you realize that you've sustained some losses. This is especially true when your intent was to hold on to everything you had. Fear surfaces for nearly everyone when they discover they need to adjust to a new world that holds no guarantees.

When anger and fear are prevailing emotions, the survival zone becomes nothing more than your personal, isolated island. And unfortunately, it's a place where millions of people choose to live out their lives. The familiar turns into survival, and the challenge and rewards of living a dynamic life disappear – if they were ever there in the first place.

But there's a *second option* available when you're confronted with discomfort in your survival zone. It involves abandoning that small, familiar island and moving on toward a new way. And it can be a challenging path for sure. But the payoff of leaving the zone and pursuing your goals makes even the biggest obstacles look manageable. Stepping beyond your survival zone will give you a life that offers you the prospect for the greatest opportunities and the richest rewards. Why? *Because outside your survival zone is where your dreams reside.*

Remember Tex saying he was "comfortable" in construction, even though he stayed with it ten years longer than he wanted to? Ultimately, Tex became one of the "lucky" ones—he made the *choice* to change. Far too many others never assert themselves enough to leave behind a way of life that no longer works for them. They simply don't step out of their survival zones to experience new relationships. They never manage to turn their fear and anger into opportunities for growth.

Just ask yourself, "Am I one of these people?" Have you given your survival zone so much control over your life that you're stuck and you'll never take the opportunity to pursue your dream?

If you're not sure, there's one question that can help put the whole issue into perspective. Ask yourself, "Am I doing what I truly want to do?" If you are, great. Congratulations! If you're not, however, your dreams are still waiting for you. Start focusing on them now. Earlier you were introduced to identifying what you truly want. So, what is it?

Finally, when was the last time you challenged yourself to step beyond the limits of your survival zone? What was the result? Abandon old ways of doing things and you'll enter a world of new rewards. It could be one of the most liberating things you'll ever do. Just look at Tex, but don't take as long as he did. Life's too short not to live it the way you want to. There's no "instant replay" in life. This is it!

Chapter 6

Build Your Relationships
to Succeed
New Associations Lead to New Opportunities

*"Only those who dare to take
that single step forward have
the chance to succeed...."*
Michael Kerrigan

Take a survey and nearly everyone you talk to will tell you they would like things to improve—their income, their time, their house, their car(s), and their home life. More, bigger, better, faster. It's just human nature.

But how many people will be open enough to tell you they want more rewarding relationships? Some, probably. But most? Probably not. It's not that they don't want to get along with people better. Hardly. They realize it's to their advantage to have more productive alliances with their spouse, kids, relatives, boss, and the neighbors next door.

When people give that shrug of indifference they're probably thinking, "Relationships are too much work. Anyway, I might get rejected. So who needs it?"

Now you may not be part of that mass of people who turn from the thought of forging new friendships and alliances. You may even be at the other end of the spectrum and hug strangers! Then again, you may not. Even if you're fairly confident in meeting new people, and regularly put yourself on the social line, it may not always be an easy experience. After all, the possibility of getting rejected is always there.

Wherever you may stand in the area of relationship-building, crafting new associations can always be made easier. Your effectiveness with others can always improve, whether you're reaching out to someone new or improving existing relationships.

Plug In

Now you may ask this: "Why do I need to concern myself with any of this?" That's easy—*to have a better life!* Just look at the news. Social splits seem to be growing deeper every day. The differences between people are exploited, not only along the lines of race, economics, and age, but also in education, politics, and religion.

Whole communities are being created behind secure walls. One recent survey showed that as many as 12 million Americans live in gated communities. It's a trend reflecting a drift toward isolation. And the way we communicate, conduct our business, and spend our leisure time is done—with increasing popularity—in isolation.

The growing use of the Internet provides just one example. Anyone can now tap into a whole new world of ideas, businesses, and trends from in front of their computer screen, and never have to physically engage another human being. Nearly everything—from conversations to airline reservations to classroom instruction—can be carried out in the privacy and solitude of our own heads.

But if your goal is to improve your relationships and your life, you need to relate with other people along the way. There's no escaping it, or them. And the more skilled you are in dealing with people—face to face—the greater your rewards will be. In fact, the more high-tech our society becomes the more high-touch we need to use in building our relationships.

Of course, you can always go another way, abandoning civility and engaging in demands and confrontations. For some, angrily communicating is their way of life. Verbal jabs—just short of physical punches—is all they know, or care to know.

A conflict-resolution seminar I attended provided an ideal forum for a wide range of relationship perspectives. One of the more candid participants, an attorney, said he was taking the course to see if he could learn to *keep his elbows in.* He admitted that threats and intimidation were his ways of doing his daily business. It was an entrenched habit of his. And he's certainly not alone.

You can probably think of a few instances where bullying and confrontation were used by one person to prevail over another. But while force and scorn may win a victory in court, they're likely to get a cold shoulder, a black eye, or some other form of rejection in everyday life.

Pass Through the Gate

In reconsidering how you're dealing with other people, focus on what I call the *Gate of Change*.

Reference to a *gate* is made simply to create a mental image. You might think of it as a threshold or passage. It represents a barrier that's preventing your ultimate success. You want to pass through it so you can discover the improved relationships that can help you in every facet of your life—from now on.

Understand that the gate can be unlatched only from one side—yours! Now you may be thinking that just about every gate you've ever seen swings both ways. So there's just as much opportunity for the person on the other side to open the gate for you as there is for you to open it for him or her. That's true.

But have you ever *waited* for someone else to act? How many times have you seen someone interesting or fun-loving and right on the mark? You may have thought, "Gee, I sure would like to get to know him or her better. I'll just wait here quietly until he or she discovers how interested I am. My silence will speak for itself."

And there you sat with that witty person never saying anything to you. Your being quiet, obviously, didn't work! He or she couldn't read your mind, so they simply vanished from your life.

How many times have you ever spotted someone like that? Those opportunities don't happen often enough to let them slip by, unaddressed. Agree? Consider just one memory you have of an encounter that *never* happened, but easily could have if you had just opened the gate for that person.

At various times, we are all presented with opportunities to take the initiative. For some, it amounts to little more than choosing to strike up a conversation. While for others, asserting themselves is quite difficult—with progress that can barely be measured.

Take Lyle, for example. He's bright and engaging, and operates in a broad circle of people. His job requires him to network constantly. On the surface, Lyle has effective relationships everywhere.

On our way to dinner one night, though, Lyle said something I didn't expect to hear. He said he was depressed over the state of his relationships, confessing that most of the people he knew were *bores*.

Now I was taking this much too personally and was about to let Lyle out of the car, when he said we could get together more often. It had been a couple of months since we had really talked. So to help him get past this depression, and to reconnect with someone in my own network, I agreed. I suggested he call me when he had time.

Two months later, a mutual friend mentioned that she thought Lyle had gone *underground*. She said it was like he no longer existed, as he had been staying away from everyone.

Later on, I called Lyle to see how he was doing and asked about getting together. He said he'd call me back before the weekend, but he never did. As much as Lyle said he wanted to establish new contacts and seek out people who might help him take his life in a new direction, he never did it.

Willingness, Ability, and Action

Passing through the *Gate of Change* means meeting some conditions, including *willingness*, *ability,* and *action*.

In Lyle's case, he said he was willing. Some people never even do *that*. They stay firmly where they are, consciously choosing *not* to reach out to anyone. Ask them if there's a chance to improve their relationships, or to meet someone new, or take on a unique challenge, and they shake their heads *no*. End of discussion.

There was no question that Lyle had the ability to make new connections. He proved it every time he picked up the phone to make a business call, or shook hands with someone for the first time. When it came to taking *action*, though, it was an entirely different story. Positive action was the missing element in Lyle's opportunity to pass through the gate.

Now look again at those three elements: willingness, ability, and action. How do they apply to you when it comes to establishing new relationships?

- Do you focus your attention on each of these steps, or do you always let something get in the way?
- Do you tell yourself that your communication ability is something less than it should be—so you can't develop relationships?
- Is willingness your missing element, so that even the desire to begin the process of relationship-building isn't even there?
- Or do you stall when it comes to taking action because you don't know where any of this relationship-building will lead?

Of course, there are no assurances of success once you start extending yourself and making new contacts. But if you don't start, you'll stay exactly where you are—in a place where meaningful new relationships don't happen. Only those who dare to take that single step forward have the chance for greater success.

I Remember You

Take about 30 seconds to clear your mind, and then think of the last new person you met—somebody you had never spoken to before. You may have seen that person from time to time, but you never made the effort to get to know them. Or they could be someone you have never seen before, but events brought the two of you together to say *hello*.

Now, think of the circumstances that brought you together:

- What were you thinking before you introduced yourself?
- More specifically, what were you thinking about that person and about yourself?
- Was it physical attraction or something the other person said that caught your attention and brought you together?
- What was your emotional reaction after you shook hands with this person and started your conversation?
- And what were you thinking five minutes into the conversation, if it lasted that long?
- If your contact was successful, how can you repeat the emotions you were feeling, the thoughts you were thinking, or the circumstances that existed when you finally met?
- If it wasn't successful, or your contact with this person didn't last more than five minutes and you wanted it to, why did it fail or dissolve so quickly?

Retrace the circumstances, your feelings, and thoughts when the contact occurred. Think about what you could have changed—your tone of voice, the questions you asked, or something else—that might have made your encounter successful. Of course, you can't control everything. Some of the responsibility for making a connection lies with the other person. The point is, though, that you *can* control much of the interaction if you really want to. Be confident of that.

While your willingness, ability, and action are essential to your meeting new people, making successful contacts also requires that you harness a wide range of senses—all at the same time. Effective interaction asks you to show interest, which means to pay attention—both to what is being said to you and by you—and respond to a range of physical and verbal cues from the person you're meeting.

Meeting new people requires you to step outside your survival zone—the area in your life that holds the people, places, things, and beliefs that you rely on. In the case of changing behaviors or pursuing new goals, how you allow the survival zone to affect you has a huge influence on your personal growth—whether you move on or stay stuck where you are.

Striving to grow beyond your survival zone without improving and expanding your relationships is virtually impossible. Whether the setting is social or business-related, growing beyond your current way of being—the limits you have set for yourself—often requires the insight and help of others. Don't be afraid to ask for it!

Beware of the "Leash"

My 11 years as a journalist gave me plenty of opportunities to observe a myriad of interactions, without even leaving the newsroom.

Between 1981 and 1992, I worked as a reporter and editor for four different publications. At the heart of each operation was the newsroom, which is a lot like a high school cafeteria—a big, cluttered, noisy hall. There's no privacy, by design. Overhearing conversations is a normal part of the operation. Spur-of-the-moment help from other reporters happens all the time. And watching people interact—especially on deadline—is part of the fun of working in this environment.

Each of these newsrooms had an array of departments—news, sports, business, features, editorial, the copy desk, and photography.

And each operated basically on its own, headed by an independent editor. It never ceased to amaze me how differently each department was run and the wide swings in the quality of work produced from one department to the next.

Without exception, the editors who allowed their reporters the most latitude in reporting and creatively writing their stories produced the best results. Those editors left *their* survival zones every day to let the reporters do new things. *Trust* is what made these relationships such a success, coupled with the fact that these editors were also willing to step through the Gate of Change.

And those *other* editors, those who kept their reporters on short "leashes" and maintained tight control of the stories, were always tormented by challenges and mistakes. There was no dialogue during conversations—only commands issued from the top. Those editors always thought they knew better than anyone else and, along with having the final word, that was the survival zone with which they were familiar. And this familiarity obviously mattered to them.

When their reporters were hired, those frustrated editors were always excited by the prospect of what was to come. But that potential was hardly ever realized because they would never surrender control. And in most cases, that's the way they had operated for years. Trust wasn't in their vocabulary, and the reporters were undermined. They could never roam very far or even come close to reaching their potential.

Now consider your own survival zone:

- Are you willing to surrender some comfort and familiarity to improve the way you're living—especially with the people around you?
- Have you tested your ability to cooperate in establishing new relationships or improving the ones you already have?
- Have you taken positive, meaningful action to make those relationships work?

Opening the Gate of Change to others is the first step in creating the relationships—and the success—you want.

Chapter 7

Risk Letting Go—And Grow
Take Action to Overcome Fear

*"Your taking action is a necessary ingredient
in overcoming any fear you may have. And the
process begins with that first step toward
your goal and that new way of being."*
Michael Kerrigan

From the time we're young, we know fear. It comes in a variety of forms—the dark, the unknown, bullies, grades, siblings, and perhaps stern parents and teachers. And most of us will do almost anything to avoid fear—*almost* anything.

As we get older, our fears graduate to more sophisticated forms of the same old stuff—rejection, humiliation, and failure. And we'll generally do whatever we can to avoid these as well.

The impact of fear—at any age—is to keep us where we are. We feel we are unable to make choices that will lift us out of the situations we're *allowing* to control us. When it comes to blocking your ability to exercise free will, fear knows exactly where you're vulnerable. Fear will play on those weaknesses—but only if you let it. Knowing where fear is likely to appear will help you defeat it.

A Lesson in Anxiety

One of fear's favorite disguises is anxiety, whether it involves a move to a new job, a different part of the country, a promising relationship, taking advantage of an opportunity, or some other change.

Jenny is no stranger to anxiety's cold touch. She's a large woman in her 40s and her size is an important element in dealing with her fear. She's about 5-feet 7-inches tall, and weighs in the neighbor-hood of 250 pounds—most of the time. That is, until she feels the inclination to have a romantic relationship. And then, slowly, her weight begins to disappear.

But as Jenny nears what she calls *the danger zone*, somewhere around 200 pounds, her weight loss stalls. The pounds that came off easily over weeks of diet and exercise dwindle into ounces. But even with this slowdown, a crisis inevitably hits. In a tone befitting a funeral, Jenny announces, "I've been asked out on a date. What am I going to do?" Occasionally, she'll go. Often, though, she won't.

As much as her romantic urge tells her to get out there and min-gle, she'll still find some way to sabotage that desire. Predictably, her anxiety over dating and its implications for a relationship be-come overwhelming. Her fear of a bond with someone she doesn't yet know wins out, and her weight returns—until the next time.

Just as Jenny lets her fear defeat her efforts at forming romantic relationships, there are other factors to help complicate things. To get what she really wants, Jenny needs to let go of some of her old ways. Otherwise she'll just continue to repeat the same behavior and get the results she doesn't want.

Take Some New Approaches

By its very nature, reaching a new goal requires adopting new, more effective methods and behaviors, while eliminating the old, ineffective ones. These new ways of behaving can become threats to you and others, just as in Jenny's case.

Heading in a new direction, with new objectives, offers fear another opportunity to step in. For many, dealing with new challenges, espe-cially without the support of others, becomes too much to cope with. As a result, they often abandon their efforts to change.

Karen was a newspaper reporter, one of the best on a staff of 100. When she was offered a promotion and a transfer to the Wash-ington, D.C. bureau, she was elated. It was the highest compliment she could have received for her work.

Karen accepted. But then she started to think through what the move *really* meant. She'd no longer have her car, which she affec-tionately called *Honey*, but would have to rely on the mass transit system and cabs.

No longer would Karen have the comfort of her familiar newsroom; she would have to file her stories from the Capitol pressroom. She would have to do her shopping at a small Korean grocery near her condominium, rather than at a large supermarket, with *Honey* waiting for her in the parking lot. And Karen would also have to leave behind her old friends, and make new ones.

The multitude of changes proved too much for her to cope with, so Karen turned down the Washington job. She made a choice. She chose to stay in her survival zone, where people, things, and procedures were familiar. It was a place where her success was virtually assured. She could continue to do the things she had always done, go to the same proven sources for her stories, and be guaranteed the comfort of her established network of friends.

Unfortunately, Karen's choice denied her the opportunity for growth. And she certainly isn't alone—tens of thousands of people make similar choices every day.

Not everyone faces the circumstances that confronted Karen. Each of us is unique, and every set of circumstances carries different priorities and possibilities. You may consider the offer of a promotion, but refuse it because of the added responsibility. You may remain unhappy in a mediocre relationship because you're afraid to confront some key issues. Or you may choose to stay in your survival zone simply out of fear of being unable to cope with something or someone new.

Choosing always involves risk. And unfortunately, most people dwell on the risk of loss—loss of friendship, loss of support, or loss of the familiar—rather than focusing on their potential for gain. And as it did with Karen, we can allow that fear to keep us locked in place, in some cases, forever.

The best way to overcome any fear you may have is simply to take action! And that begins with the first step you take toward your goal. Just start doing something to make it happen.

You *Can* Pay the Price of Success, *or* You *Will* Pay the Price of Failure!

At the other end of the choice spectrum is another risk—the risk of winning. And as attractive as winning sounds, if you don't take action it, too, can act as a mental barrier to keep you stuck. Ironically, it could keep you just as stuck as you might have been by the fear of losing!

Winning brings with it its own challenges. People may treat you differently, and expectations are likely to increase. You'll probably be counted on to perform at a higher level in everything you do.

The challenge of moving on will cause you to expand your survival zone—so you can deal with the new people and situations you'll be encountering. It's just a part of navigating the waves of change leading to your success.

Taking action to overcome any fears you may have and reaching toward success is *your* choice. It's the choice between reaching your potential or walking away and never exploring who you really are or the person you can ultimately become. And if you don't choose to pay the price of success, you'll automatically pay the price of failure—by default!

Now let's put any fears you may have into perspective. Simply think of an opportunity you may have had recently that you chose not to take advantage of because of some fear. You may have been afraid of failure, loss, rejection, or not achieving what you truly wanted.

Now ask yourself these four questions:

- If you were given the same choice today, knowing what you now know, how would you handle the opportunity?
- Would you make the same choice?
- Would the same fear prevent you from taking advantage of the opportunity?
- Could you possibly make the same mistake twice?

Learning from your experiences is one of the most valuable lessons you can have. Just be sure you're paying attention when the lesson—*and the opportunity*—arise! Remember, luck happens when opportunity and preparedness meet.

Chapter 8

The Not-So-Great Escape
Go for Freedom to Fulfill Your Goal

*"Our individual Bill of Rights can serve as the structure
for our own personal empowerment—to live effectively with change
while exercising responsible choices as we go."*
Michael Kerrigan

L ook around and you'll discover change is inevitable. From
the vehicles we drive and the clothes we wear, to the technology that helps us on the job or in our business, change
is rampant.

When it comes to man-made objects, change seems natural. But
when it comes to people, the story takes a dramatic turn. Change is
viewed as everything from wonderful, to a hurdle, to a curse. The
survival zone has a lot to do with it. Many people simply don't want
to change their familiar behaviors and surroundings. But the issue
runs even deeper than that—it concerns exerting themselves and
taking responsibility.

Erich Fromm, in his mid-Twentieth Century study of authoritar-
ian governments, called the act of denying responsibility as an
escape from freedom. Sadly, millions of people still give their freedom away every day just to avoid the discomfort that may be
triggered by taking responsibility. In their efforts to avoid responsibility for their behavior, people give control of their lives over to
someone or something else.

This otherwise personal responsibility is turned over to a wife, a husband, a boss, or a corporation. In essence, those who give their freedom away say, "You know how my life should be lived better than I do, so tell me what to do. I give up." In essence, they surrender—without even a single objection!

Take a minute and think back to a war movie you probably saw as a kid. There, filling the screen, is a full-fledged battle—with guns and bayonets, and explosions everywhere. But suddenly, the fighting stops. Out of a crack in the crumbling fortress wall appears a white flag, dangling at the end of a stick. It's the flag of surrender.

Shortly afterward, with hands raised above their heads, the exhausted soldiers emerge from the building. The struggle of the fight shows on their faces as they walk toward their enemy, defeated. And the screen fades to black.

Now imagine the scenes you witness every day, whether it's at a crowded factory, a teeming office building, the isolation of a rural farm, or somewhere else. Disillusioned workers, their faces somber with the look of quiet resignation and lost hope, are going through the paces that make up their lives.

Others aren't so passive. They appear on the highway, cutting off other drivers, their faces twisted with rage; or in the office, attacking coworkers with sarcasm and ridiculing their performances. These scenes are repeated by millions of people, day in and day out. Undoubtedly, many of them think how different life could be. But they create an ocean of excuses in which they can swim away from their responsibilities to themselves and their families.

This is their first lie—they believe they are not responsible.

A Longing for Personal Freedom

A longing for personal freedom distinguishes the drama of defeat in everyday life from the battle in the war movie. The movie characters surrender only after a high-pitched battle in the face of overwhelming odds and impending doom. It's quite different for most employees in factories, offices, and on farms and other such places—who willingly give up their freedom. There are rarely any bullets. There is no physical fight, nor are they taking much, if any, positive action on their own behalf. But for many who surrender, the voice saying how different life could be simply doesn't go away.

This is the second lie—the lie of delay. And it's the deadliest form of denial.

Tex, the llama rancher, took ten years to decide to finally leave a job he'd grown tired of and begin a new career. There was no guarantee he would ultimately have the chance to pursue his dream or make it a reality. He got "lucky" because he took action.

How many people, in the middle of a job, profession, or relationship they can barely tolerate, tell themselves that sooner or later they'll do whatever it takes to make things better? They run from freedom while telling themselves they'll someday be brave and take responsibility. But circumstances change. The unforeseeable happens. Layoffs, injuries, divorce, and death can, and do, intervene. The lie of delay wins and someday turns into never.

So the next time you get on the highway entry ramp, or file into your office building, school, factory, or other work location, perhaps with 1,000 coworkers, take a long look at the people around you. Are they fulfilled, or are they simply going through the motions of survival? Are their hands raised in defeat?

Now look at yourself. Are your hands raised as well? Or are you going to do what you need to do to give yourself the life you want?

Exert Your Rights

If you think there's a better, more fulfilling way to live, it's time to do so. Exercise your free will and embrace your personal Bill of Rights.

The first ten amendments to the United States Constitution make up our civil Bill of Rights, including the right to free speech, to keep and bear arms, and to a trial by jury, among others. Some people take these rights for granted, while others practice them with conviction.

But what I believe to be of equal importance to U.S. constitutional protections, are the rights that each of us has in living our own lives. Our individual Bill of Rights can serve as the structure for our own personal empowerment—to live effectively with change and while exercising responsible choices in the process.

The six pillars of that personal Bill of Rights include:

- The right to live the way you choose, without harming others.

- The right to leave behind those who don't encourage or support your efforts.
- The right to change your behavior in seeking a life that's more productive and satisfying to you.
- The right to give yourself a belief system that nurtures you.
- The right to abandon any ideas that run contrary to your best interests.
- The right to associate with those who respect your integrity and help you achieve your full potential.

If you haven't thought about exercising your freedom of choice and taking back your personal rights, start now. Stop handing them over to someone else, regardless of who it may be.

Chapter 9

Write Your Own Programs
It's Time to Be Who You Are

> *"Each generation predominantly
> relies on the last to provide them with
> the basis of their worldview. And now that
> string of folktales and porch wisdom
> resides with you."*
> Michael Kerrigan

L ook in the mirror, and who do you see? A word of caution: You may not be alone!

You're probably saying to yourself, "I know good and well who's going to be looking back without my looking, thank you."

But look anyway. Of course it's going to be you in the mirror's reflection. But look closer. Whose eyes do you have? Whose mouth did you inherit? What about the shape of your face and the mole in the middle of your forehead—where did those come from? The face looking back in the mirror isn't just you. You'll see traces of your father, your mother, a hint of your Uncle Monty or Aunt Shirley.

And the traits you get from these other people influence more than just your physical appearance. Your attitudes, beliefs, prejudices, and programs have also been bestowed upon you, whether you like them or not. Keeping them, you'll discover, is another matter *entirely*. In the meantime, it's important for you to know that your mental programs—the internal software you live your life with—is largely someone *else's* doing.

This programming, which affects the way you think, choose, and respond, begins early in life. The programs start with the lullaby you heard as an infant and filter into each crevice of who you are. The programs continue to pour in over dinner table conversations, during rides in the car, and with scoldings, praise, and simple explanations of the way the world works.

Programs leave you with a package of attitudes and beliefs, and provide you with a basis for dealing with everyone else. And as traditional and widespread as this method of social imprinting is, there's a challenge: Much of it is flawed. One estimate holds that up to three-quarters of our programming is either negative or the wrong kind.

Most people are programmed to follow the crowd, play it safe, and not stand out. But people who do this, at the same time, are stifling who they are and what they can really contribute as well as their success, happiness, and fulfillment.

Imagine that three-quarters of the software you bought for your personal computer didn't work like it was supposed to. It was printing out as fact that Paris is the capital of California, and that $1 + 1 = 1$ million. How long would it take you to go to or call the place where you bought this program and demand your money back?

Unfortunately, when it comes to ourselves, we may not be nearly so quick to respond. We may drag our feet in correcting our occasional tics and misfirings. Too often we may not bother to straighten out those twists in performance and logic that complicate our lives. In essence, we accept that Paris has replaced Sacramento as California's capital city, and we don't think anything more about it.

Where Did You Get *That?*

Now consider this whole scenario of information transfer from a historical perspective. Let's say you were brought up by your parents. From where did your parents—the teachers who likely influenced your thinking the most—get *their* thinking? Exactly—from your grandparents! Each generation predominately relies on the last to provide them with the basis of their thinking and their worldview. And now that string of folktales and porch wisdom resides within you.

By now, you might be saying to yourself, "I'd never repeat my parents' mistakes. I'd never embrace their prejudices or biases or old-fashioned ideas. I'm my own person." And on a conscious level, you're probably right. You may not think that all laborers are inferior, that all politicians are crooked, or that a single drink makes someone an alcoholic.

But so much for conscious thought. The real challenges reside in your subconscious thoughts and actions. We all operate automatically relying on this stored knowledge—our programs, so to speak. Just as a computer provides instantaneous bits of information from its database, so does your brain.

Your *programs* click in when you see a stranger walking toward you on the street, or when you merely hear some current political name or buzzword. Your *programs* can tell you that the approaching stranger is going to attack, when, in fact, that person is just sharing the sidewalk. Or that the political speaker, rather than endorsing a radical person or idea, is mentioning them simply to make a larger, reasonable point.

But the *programming* you have received over time and stored, in most cases, gives you just one option. You access the program in your brain and the program may say that stranger's going to attack.

Unfortunately, the *choices* you make can be no better than the *programs* you have behind them. But these programs can be generations out of date and no longer valid—if they *ever* made sense for you. And while you can change your programs, it requires some new thinking.

You Are What You Think

The first, most effective step you can take to change your programs is to give some thought to your *personal philosophy*. Make a conscious decision about how you want to live your life. Figure out what's important to you, personally and emotionally. Determine what kind of person you're going to be, and how you're going to interact most effectively with others.

This personal philosophy can be as simple as a few words or a sentence. It may be to:

- Treat myself with greater respect.

- Exercise greater understanding of others.
- Always strive to do my best.

Now determine if the programs you're carrying around with you are consistent with that philosophy. But since it would take hours or days to review all of your attitudes and measure their worth against this life goal, don't bother. Your programs will surface soon enough as you interact with others in your daily routine. And if you discover that your programs and the ways in which you deal with others conflict with the philosophy you've written down, change the programs that don't apply anymore.

Making the choice to think and act more effectively is up to you. And changing your programs is the place to start. Just because you look like Uncle Monty doesn't mean you have to act like him, too.

Change the Channel

Think of one program you got from your parents or someone else who had a big impact on you as you grew up. We all carry these programs around with us, and they're as clear and distinct as hearing your mother's advice come out of *your* mouth.

Again, this program could involve the way you regard success, the way you invest your money (or don't), or some other trait that was handed down to you that you're living with—gladly, reluctantly, or unconsciously.

Now, look at that program more closely by asking yourself these questions:

- Is it consistent with your personal philosophy?
- Is keeping this program helping you get to where you want to go?
- What philosophical adjustments could you make to help you operate more effectively?
- Would it be best to abandon the program completely and start over with one that will help you live the life you want?

It's your life and your choice. You decide.

Chapter 10

Beware of *Great* Advice
Encourage Yourself to Achieve Your Dreams

*"In too many cases people are
more than willing to surrender their own
decision-making power to someone else....
They have yet to develop the confidence in themselves
that they are capable of making excellent choices."*
Michael Kerrigan

The world is filled with people who are more than willing to tell you what to do with your life. These self-appointed advisors come from all backgrounds and disciplines—psychiatrists and sociologists, parents, friends, strangers, and almost anyone you can think of.

They're all anxious to tell you what profession or business to select, which mate to choose, which investments are appropriate, and why what you're doing now is probably *wrong*. They're all ready to pass judgment and make your choices for you.

But in the end, it's *you* who needs to decide your own course. It's you who needs to sort it all out and do what you believe is best for you. Sure, others can give you ideas, but the bottom line is, it's *your* life. After all, your friends don't pay your bills! This step toward self-reliance not only makes sense, it's absolutely necessary.

You have more information about yourself than anyone else, including your parents, your partner, and your kids. Other people can give you feedback based only upon the information you're willing to share.

In essence, you are your own resource library.

- You alone know your thoughts and perceptions of the way the world works.
- Only you know the slights and prejudices you encountered growing up, as well as the joys and intimate moments you hold close to your heart.
- And you alone know why you're willing to embrace or reject certain people, places, and beliefs.

So, who better than you to give yourself comfort, encouragement, and goals? Think about it.

Now this isn't a suggestion that you dismiss everything everyone else has to say. Relying on others for information, perspective, and new ideas can be invaluable—as long as they are positive-thinking people and their suggestions are offered to help you move ahead. A mentor or leader with whom you regularly counsel may be a great resource for you to help you stay on track and more forward.

No matter what, though, always turn to yourself first when you're faced with a challenge or have a dream. You often know in your heart what you need to do. Don't surrender your own decision-making power to someone else. Know you *are* capable of making choices.

And don't be afraid of what you might tell yourself. Remember, we typically look out for our own best interests first. As long as you're honest with yourself, the likelihood you'll steer yourself wrong is almost zero.

As direct as this approach may be, though, it can be one of the most challenging roads to take. Millions of people spend years deceiving themselves into thinking they are getting what they want, or that somehow they don't deserve their dream.

Be Selective

Dave's an exception. He's 27 and in the construction business with his father. He's had plenty of advice about what to do with his life. The prevailing attitude among his coworkers is, "Stay where you are."

But construction *isn't* his passion. Driving racing cars *is*. And Dave has certainly won enough races to begin making a name for himself. However, his racing career is at a critical juncture. Dave either finds the money and backers to pursue his dream, or he walks away. And while it wouldn't be fun, it would certainly be easy for him to turn his back on racing. For most people, quitting on the pursuit of their dream is all too easy an option to take.

Building and maintaining a racing career is challenging, no doubt about it. But racing is the easy part. Dave must also get involved in an ongoing quest for money for support and for time to race. But he's not about to let circumstances have their way with his choice.

"I hear it every day," he says, with no hint of sympathy. "These guys who work construction are burned out in their 40s and 50s, and they look at me and say, 'When I was your age, I could have done this, I should have done that, or I once had the chance to...' whatever.

"But they didn't do it. And here they are, pounding nails or hauling bricks, wishing they had done something else. I never want to be in that situation," Dave concludes. "I'm not going to look back on my life and say I wish I had done this or that. I'm going to have done it."

While he hasn't yet achieved the success he wants, Dave is still living his dream. In casual conversation he rates the differences between the go-carts he learned to race in and the larger, more powerful car he now drives. He confesses that his fear melts into excitement as he reaches speeds of 120 miles an hour--through a curve! He describes how he's grown more comfortable pushing himself beyond his perceived limits.

Dave talks about *growing* toward his goal. He doesn't have the time or patience for people telling him what to do with his life. They have their own success—or failure—to deal with. Dave has his. And *you* have your own!

Take a Message

Take a minute to think about the way you advise yourself. Think of the array of situations you encounter when your internal voice clears its throat and starts talking.

That advice can take the form of a running debate that weighs the positive, negative, and neutral sides of some situation you're dealing with. That voice can also surface in words of encouragement or discouragement. And unfortunately, it often presents itself in words and phrases of regret—*If only I had....*

Regardless of what form that voice takes, think about what you tell yourself and how you say it. Think of two examples of the self-counseling you already do:

- First, consider an example of negative words you might be saying to yourself.
- Second, think of an example of positive counseling you do for yourself.
- Finally, ask yourself where these two self-counseling approaches have gotten you.

Have you ever talked yourself into a corner with discouraging self-talk like, "I won't make it. I'll fail"? Now think of specific situations in which you talked yourself through to success with encouragement by saying, "I can do it. I'm going to make it."

If you find that taking suggestions from others is still important to you—and it *could* be—here's a tool you can use to help capture the very best advice when it's tossed your way. The next time someone offers you his or her wisdom about how you should be living your life, give it a simple reality test. Look at how they're living their lives, then ask yourself these three questions:

- Are they doing what *they* want?
- Are they fulfilled by what *they're* doing?
- Are they successful by *your* standards?

If the answer to each is *yes*, you may want to consider what the advice giver has to say. Otherwise, you may want to think twice about acting on their unsolicited wisdom.

Remember Dave, the racecar driver? He got advice all the time, but he didn't allow it to interfere with the pursuit of his goal. He encouraged himself to achieve the dream *he* wanted.

Chapter 11

From Here to Your Dreams
Master Your Roadmaps and Self-Talk Scripts

"We all talk to ourselves. It's human nature.
It used to be said that talking to yourself was a
sign of insanity. Not many people are
saying that anymore."
Michael Kerrigan

Remember your last road trip? Not the one to the newest mall, but a long journey that took you to a place you had never been before. What was the first thing you did in preparation after pulling out the map?

More than likely, you found your destination. And then you started plotting the course to get there. It was a systematic move that made a lot of sense. And you probably arrived at where you wanted to go with the smallest amount of hassle.

When it comes to pursuing your dreams, this same logical approach is the most efficient way to get there. So let's examine the act of pursuing what you want.

The first step is to select a goal. The next step is to plot your course—just like that road trip. As best-selling author Stephen R. Covey suggests, you're going to *begin with the end in mind.* Identifying your goal is, essentially, locating your destination on the map. Spotting where you're going will help you to get, and stay, focused.

The empowering thing about this trip is that *you* control reaching your goal. You can get off the road and get back on whenever you choose, without losing sight of where you're headed. You regulate the direction, the approach, and the pace.

For some, the road to their goal meanders like a river, cutting back and forth across flat, uneventful terrain. Occasionally, the landscape is friendly, comprised only of safe, productive environments. At other times it is unfriendly, revealing places that are sometimes pointless, unhealthy, and even life-threatening.

For others, the road plots a straight line—from life's beginning to its inevitable, predictable end. The course never waivers to the left or right. It pauses infrequently, allowing little time to think and reflect. Still other roads fall somewhere in between the meandering path and the single straight-line expressway.

Beginning with the end in mind doesn't mean you get to your goal without the chance to really live life along the way—on the contrary. *Knowing where you're going and pursuing it will give you added opportunities to live life more fully.* If you need to take a time-out along the way to a goal you truly want, you'll have the motivation to get back on the road with renewed enthusiasm and desire.

Here, There, Everywhere, and Nowhere

Phil is just one of many examples of a person unmotivated by a goal, traveling down a road that took him everywhere and nowhere at the same time. He attended a large Texas university, where he was torn between journalism and politics. During his senior year, he served as editor of the school's newspaper. His dedication to journalism was unsurpassed. A career devoted to free speech seemed assured—until graduation, that is.

Then Phil headed to a college in Wisconsin to pursue a master's degree in political science. After his graduation, he moved to Washington, D.C., to serve on the staff of a high-profile member of the U.S. Senate. From all appearances, Phil had made a successful entry into the political arena, which was the direction he had chosen. Then, undoubtedly surprising to some, he enrolled in another master's program, this time at a university in Virginia, for yet another degree in journalism.

After his third graduation, Phil moved back to Texas, taking a job with a major newspaper. It seemed like he had come home to the First Amendment and daily deadlines. After five years, he was transferred back to Washington to cover politics.

By the time Phil turned 40, he had left the newspaper, but remained in Washington to work for a trade publication. The trouble was he was tired of journalism and cynical about politics. Ask him what his goal was and he'd give you a blank stare that said, "Don't ask." Phil conceded that his real goal never was to be a reporter or a politician, much less to work in a politician's office!

The road he took to reach a goal he never identified was full of fits and starts. His journey was one that darted back and forth and ultimately led to something he never wanted.

Now you may be asking where's the happy ending? In Phil's case, there isn't one—yet. He says he's working on it, though. I tell you about Phil because what he's gone through illustrates two points:

- The first is to *pursue a goal or dream you want*. What that is may not be apparent to you now, but through persistent, careful consideration and honest deliberation with yourself it will surface.
- The second point is to *get on the road that will bring you to your dream or goal*. It's easy to find diversions, especially if you're heading in a direction you don't want to go. Phil found plenty of them.

Are You Listening to Yourself?

Now self-talk scripts play a different role than roadmaps, although they're closely aligned. Self-talk scripts are what you tell yourself along the way. They consist of that internal dialogue, which could be either encouraging or discouraging, that you rely on to get from one point to the next on the road to your dream.

We all talk to ourselves—it's human nature. And while it used to be said that talking to yourself was a sign of insanity, most people aren't saying that anymore. And with larger numbers of people becoming more isolated in their work, the only person some people can *find* to talk to is themselves.

So when was the last time you overheard someone on the street, in the grocery store, or in your workplace, say something to him or herself? Was it positive, designed to encourage that person to strive for excellence or congratulate him or her for a job well done? Or was it a self-defeating slam, meant to reprimand him or her for some minor offense—real or imagined? And how about *you*?

- When was the last time you talked to yourself?
- What did you say, or weren't you paying attention?

All too often, our self-talk is negative and damaging. I can only imagine the scripts that Phil was using to get himself from one point in his life to the next. "Do this, do that. Be this, be that. You can do this. You can't do that. Is this what I really want? Yes! No!" Who wouldn't end up confused and unfocused with messages that were so mixed? As I said, I never delved too deeply into what Phil was really about. I respected his look that simply said, "Don't ask."

When you're reprogramming yourself and writing new self-talk scripts, tell yourself enthusiastically that you can accomplish what you set out to do. Then consistently encourage yourself until you achieve it. When you're moving forward, keep your destination in perspective at all times.

Now let's cast some light on your past behaviors and help lay the groundwork for more constructive actions in the future—including both your maps *and* scripts. Ask yourself:

- When was the last time you questioned one of your behaviors?
- What motivated you to even notice your actions?
- What did you finally do about it?
- How did that change your map?
- How did you adjust your script?
- How are you encouraging yourself now?

If you think there's a better way for you to deal with other people or situations, chart a new course for your behavior. Consider writing yourself a new script to help bolster your new actions.

If you're satisfied with the way your life is going, content with the map you have, congratulations. Take some time to consider the course you're following and the self-talk you're using as reference points for pursuing your *next* goal or dream.

If things could be better, take stock of what you're doing and assess why your life's not working the way you want it to. Life's certainly a journey, but it doesn't have to be an aimless one. Give yourself the roadmaps and scripts that will make it a journey well worth taking.

Chapter 12

Tame Your Trolls
Get Rid of Negative Influences

*"Anyone who is on the verge of a new course
in life knows that there is always the prospect of
a better way—of behaving, of thinking,
of relating to others."*
Michael Kerrigan

Until we reach the age of about seven, the only trolls most of us know live under bridges in children's books. And then things change.

Trolls emerge in real life and never seem to go away. They surface at school, at work, even at home. And just like the trolls in the *Three Billy Goats Gruff*, they stand in the way of your progress and dreams. And taking back your life becomes more of a challenge than you had probably ever imagined.

While you may not remember all the specifics of the Billy Goats' challenge, that's okay. The story's a little outdated. A current-day troll tale might go something like this:

Once upon a time there was a group of friends. Three buddies from college, who, as the twists and turns of life would have it, all landed jobs in the same town after graduation.

Mark worked as an accountant, John, as a computer programmer, and Clarence, as an artist. They were pals. Not friends, really, but pals. They knew each other well enough, and well enough was as far as it went.

As pals often do, they moved into a house together—just as they had in college. And even though they didn't always see eye-to-eye and had different perspectives on many things, they formed a pact.

But those areas of disagreement were either glossed over or ignored. After all, the threat of a disagreement could interfere with their relationship. It could split the pact, and send them on their separate ways. But living together was cheap, and cheap meant good. So they put up with each others' little quirks. They went to their jobs, lived under the same roof, and talked about their college days.

An Awakening Occurs

Then one day, John, the computer programmer, uttered something he had never said before. John told Clarence, the artist, and Mark, the accountant, that he no longer wanted to be a programmer. John told the others that he wanted to *bake cakes*.

"Bake cakes!" shouted Clarence. "You're a programmer. You don't know anything about baking cakes. Cakes are baked by big fat guys with donut breath. And women!" Clarence continued. "The last time I noticed, you were about 150 pounds and your breath smelled like mint toothpaste. And you aren't a woman, are you?"

Mark, the accountant, took a different tack indeed.

"Yeah, finished cakes are going for about $20 a pop," he estimated. "Now, from box to mixing bowl, through the oven process and frosting, is about two hours. With measuring, mixing, and cleaning up, I figure you can't do anymore than three cakes at a time: that's $60 in two hours, or $30 an hour.

"Now, let's deduct ingredients, overhead, health insurance, rent, and your car payment. And, if my calculations are right, you're operating in the hole," Mark continued. "Oh, yeah, there's still your college loan hanging around like an old girlfriend."

"Get a clue," advised Mark, with more than a hint of contempt. "Stay with programming."

Turning Over Control

And John, who had never bucked popular opinion or, more important to him, the opinions of his pals, stayed in programming. And he told himself that it was okay. It's a good profession. Computers are everywhere. Programmers are in demand.

"I'll have enough money to do what I want," he thought. "And I won't gain weight and have donut breath. And that other thing," he panicked, "I can still be a guy! Man, what was I thinking?"

And John became a good programmer. He never created his own software, but he was great at tweaking the programs of others to get them running just right. He made a nice living as a programmer, and bought a house and took vacations when he wanted to. But he always lived his life with that *unfulfilled dream* of baking cakes.

"And that's okay," John reasoned. "My pals wouldn't tell me I was wrong unless I was wrong. Would they?"

Wolves and Sheep

To understand their resistance to John, it's helpful to look at his pals. Mark, the accountant, really didn't want to be an accountant. Sure, he knew a debit from a credit, could work the numbers, and knew his spread sheets. But his dad had been an accountant and had always provided for his family. "It's a stable life," Dad always told him. "Be an accountant." And so Mark was.

Clarence, on the other hand, had grown tired of his brushes and paints. He wanted to travel and see the landscapes he was now only creating on canvas. He really wanted to go to a third world country and volunteer as a missionary. The fact that he had no idea which country to go to or what exactly he'd do made little difference. It was a nice idea, and Clarence held it close.

But the pressure to paint, to pursue his art, was always there. It was there from the sacrifices his parents had made to pay for his education to Clarence himself. "I will be a great artist," he told himself and his friends. "And to be a great artist, you must paint."

So Clarence was stuck. And he took great comfort from the fact that Mark was stuck too.

So when Clarence and Mark heard John utter the word *dream*, it was too much. Just like their parents who were bringing pressure to bear on them, they brought pressure down on John. Their actions said, "Dreams aren't real, so forget them."

But, in fact, Mark, the accountant, and Clarence, the artist, did realize a new calling. They became John's trolls. And they achieved that status through mockery and ridicule, as well as the more subtle approaches of innuendo and doubt.

Now the signs that Mark and Clarence might be trouble for John came early in their relationship. The fact there were things they couldn't talk about without arguing—without a rift forming in their relationships—offered the first clue. The fact they had never formed a real friendship in college could well have been another sign that sharing new information and goals might cause a bad situation.

Their interactions were peppered with judgment and second-guessing. Excitement for each other's plans and reinforcement of their goals simply didn't exist. Caution signs were everywhere.

This doesn't mean dreams and goals are not to be shared. They are! Honesty and brainstorming with others often provides valuable insight. Just make sure you know the people you're sharing your ideas with and whether they care enough about you to support you in accomplishing your dreams. Ultimately the trolls will find out what you're thinking. But let them learn of your plans only after you've decided what is truly best for you. Don't let the trolls suck the life from your dreams and goals or you'll never achieve them.

Here a Troll, There a Troll

Now, trolls can come in any age and size—and from all walks of life. Clarence and Mark represent the faction of young trolls, operating out of an absolute sense of right and wrong. For these people, perception stands in for experience when it comes to making up their minds. But simply having experience is no guarantee that you or others will exercise wisdom. Age offers no guarantee of making smart choices or giving good advice. There are plenty of trolls lurking out there with decades of experience. Among their standard response to new opportunities is, "It won't work,"—based largely on their own failings!

"I've been there," "I've tried it," "I know," are standard phrases in the arsenal of old, experienced trolls. Their criticism is usually followed by a sly smirk and a cynical shake of the head. The reaction is laden with the message, "How could you possibly succeed where I failed? Who do you think you are?"

Often, the motivation of trolls is to keep you locked in place within *their* survival zone—so you don't get ahead of them! They don't want anyone making waves and causing them to think that they're not really as happy or satisfied as they pretend to be.

It's not unusual for the people who criticize your dreams to rely on you to keep their lives sane and predictable. They want to keep you where you are. *Your* change triggers a disturbance in the way *their* world works. For them, your behavior should follow a pattern. For them, your past *is* your potential. But anyone who is on the verge of a new path in life knows there is *always* the prospect of a better way—of behaving, thinking, relating to others, and living life.

Front and Center

Now consider the trolls in your life. As you've just seen, part of identifying them is being aware of their behavior, and pinpointing the negative acts directed at you. With each troll you identify, think of his or her contrary, undermining behavior.

Finally, think of ways in which you can bring these trolls around to your way of thinking. This final step—which may appear to be a waste of time—is an important move toward alliance building. If you can begin to establish meaningful, productive associations with those people you don't always see eye-to-eye with, putting together new, more positive relationships with the people you already know and respect will be that much easier.

If you're stuck—if you can't think of any personal trolls—consider all the different areas of your life.

Start at work. Are some coworkers always running down the quality of your work, criticizing your ideas, or fighting your decisions? They may be trying to build themselves up to win a promotion or a raise. Or it could be an attempt to lock you in place, so can't reach the next level on your own ladder of growth.

Next, look at your relationships at home. Examine the behaviors of your parents, your spouse, and your children. Are they always positive around you? Is their cautionary advice meant to bring you back down to earth safely, or is the intent to hold you in place—indefinitely—until they're ready to let you proceed with your life?

Now look at your other associations. You may belong to an organization where your relationships are rocky or not as smooth as they could be. Look at the possible motivations for the negative behavior that's coming your way. Know who to confide in and from where the feedback you need will come. It's part of forming rewarding relationships and moving toward your dreams and goals.

Chapter 13

Create Your Own Reality
Imagine Life as You'd Like It to Be

*"Not being assured of the outcome you want
can act as an anchor to your current circumstances. But
it's an anchor from which every one of us – who sincerely desires
a better life – can cut ourselves free."*
Michael Kerrigan

Go to a park, or a beach, or anywhere kids congregate and play. What are they doing? What games are they creating? What characters are they inventing?

What you're likely to see are kids taking the roles of superhuman, superpowerful beings who are ten steps ahead of everyone else. These children are defining and developing themselves to accomplish any challenge imaginable.

On the playground, behavior is motivated by unlimited possibilities—because it comes without risk. As uncertain as the consequences may be for the make-believe characters, once the game's over, it's forgotten.

But as kids get older, the atmosphere changes. The rules of the game increase, are more restrictive, and are increasingly defined by parents, and then teachers, and finally, employers. And the kids' ability to create their own reality slips from their hands. Almost instantly, they're transformed into adults. The animated behavior that was typical on the playground, park, and beach disappears.

Adult-type risks—perceived and real—take the place of imaginary challenges, and they aren't so easily forgotten. Granted, the consequences are much greater when we move from the playground to the cubicle. A paycheck hinges on the outcomes.

But the fact remains, as we age, our behaviors usually become more controlled, despite our urge to create characters with youthful enthusiasm. That yearning for a creative release is often funneled into hobbies or sports practiced on weekends or at night—if then.

Real work demands different, more regimented behavior. Or so we're told. And we're taught as much by direct orders and nonverbal cues, as much as by policy manuals. And if we persist in pushing the limits—to create a reality for ourselves with more options and fewer restrictions—we usually get branded as non-conformists or troublemakers.

Sure, there are some environments where blue jeans and long hair are accepted. Most of these can be found in computer companies, or in information technology departments, where creativity is a must and arbitrary rules play less of a role.

Sadly though, rigid rules still haunt a good portion of adult behaviors and the creative process suffers as a result. And unfortunately, as many people get older they look to themselves less and less to create the atmosphere they need to succeed and be happy. Or they stop seeking places or opportunities in which they can reach their greatest potential. But it doesn't have to be that way.

Make a Wish

Take a minute and remember the Tom Hanks character in the movie *Big*. Josh, a kid of 12, goes to the amusement park and is granted one wish by an automated, plastic genie. His dream is to be big. And by the next morning his wish is granted. Physically, Josh is an adult. But inside that exterior is the 12-year-old who whispered his hope only hours before.

For much of the rest of the movie, Josh lives a fantasy life. He rises to the top of a toy company, with the latitude and opportunity to create anything he wants. He's driven by a 12-year-old's heart, will, and desire. He creates a world filled with choices and opportunities that most of us have imagined, but haven't come close to pursuing.

The problem is that many of us get in our own way. We tell ourselves that in order to behave responsibly, we must do what others expect of us. We strive to fulfill the expectations of other people, often to be disappointed because what we do or create doesn't fulfill our own expectations.

The truth is, responsible behavior is found in spending and investing your life the way *you* choose. Now you may be thinking, *that's pretty irresponsible.* After all, you have obligations to a spouse, your children, your job or business, and to an array of other people and things. And this raises a fundamental issue that each of us needs to address for ourselves—who are you living *for*?

We all have obligations—that's for sure. And to turn our backs on those relationships on a selfish whim *would* be irresponsible.

But the path to a new life isn't always as simple as black and white, yes or no. Others do play a role in how you live and, ultimately, how you're able to manage your journey. Admittedly, we're social animals. To divorce ourselves from other people, dismissing their opinions and reactions as unimportant, is unreasonable.

Networks and support *are* important. So you'll need to prepare others for your new direction. Often, those you know will be supportive. The family and friends you have in place don't want to lose you. And they'll do what they can to keep your love and friendship. In other cases, people will resist your efforts to redefine who and what you are—some so much, you'll need to leave them behind!

For many people contemplating change, the biggest obstacle to their succeeding is what psychiatrist and author M. Scott Peck calls their *will to grow.* This *will* is made up of the determination to step away from regimented behaviors and toward a life potentially much greater and rewarding.

It takes courage, step by step, to pursue this richer life because there are no guarantees of success. Not being assured of the outcome you want can act as an anchor to your current circumstances. But it's an anchor from which every one of us—who sincerely desires a better life—can cut ourselves free.

The motivation to move on to realize your dreams and goals begins with an idea. It is sparked by your childlike urge to create something new and exciting for you—something you might not have experienced in years.

Chapter 14

ADAPT Is a Positive Word
Reach Out to New Challenges

*"Committing and acting are standard ways of
behaving when you're three years old and nearly every
experience on an any given day is new as you consistently
move forward. Adapting means growth, but growth can be a scarce
resource once we become adults."*
Michael Kerrigan

At one time or another, we all tend to get a little rigid. Actions that were once fluid and natural are taken more reluctantly. And, finally, we don't take them anymore.

This progression from, *I can't wait!* to *I will not!* can be seen in the story of Theresa. She stands tentatively at the edge of the pool and looks down past the surface of the water. It's as if she's gazing into the mouth of a churning volcano. Theresa is three.

She's barely paying attention to the swimming instructor, who's down below holding out her own arms, encouraging the little girl to come into the water. This is Theresa's first time at the pool. It's foreign territory—like shoes, a spoon, and life without a diaper once were.

Her reluctance is only temporary, though. Theresa hasn't missed the splashing and laughing of her twin sister, Megan, and their four-year-old friend Kevin. The mystery of the water is overcome by Theresa's curiosity, and she commits herself to the arms of her teacher, and to swimming. She *adapts* to a new situation—a situation that, while it looks attractive, holds no guarantees.

Committing and acting are standard ways of behaving when you're three years old. Nearly every experience you have on any given day is new, as you consistently grow and move forward. *Adapting to change means growth, but growth can be a scarce resource once we become adults.*

It's Not My Style

Ed, on the other hand, can't be enticed into sampling the newest item in the produce section of the grocery store. It's a cross between an apple and a pear.

Ed likes apples, but he also likes pears. And Ed knows the difference. He's been around—for 80 years!

"What's the point?" Ed demands. "They're just trying to sell me something I don't need. There's nothing wrong with the way apples and pears have always been."

But this food evolution isn't Ed's only complaint. Actually, he's got quite a few of them, and most of his objections concern the way things have changed. Ed resents feeling he has to adapt to those changes. He thinks he has adapted quite enough, and just doesn't want to do it anymore!

Ed changed to accommodate a Depression, a World War, and a couple of smaller wars. He adjusted to new political movements, flag burning, and women taking over half the jobs in the U.S. As far as Ed's concerned, adapting is giving up and giving in. He's simply not going to give up anymore. And he's certainly not going to give in to a new fruit.

There's an issue involved, far outweighing the fact that he might like what he tastes—had he given it a chance. And taking that *chance* is the issue—that open-minded willingness to risk what you haven't experienced before.

Chance lures some into embracing change and experiencing a great benefit. But chance also drives many people into hiding or resistance— or it simply drives them away.

The chance that you might like what you'll experience may lead you to wade into the water—or maybe even jumping right in. But the chance that you may *dislike* something new can keep you from tasting the hybrid of an apple and a pear, or something else that you would really like.

You're Never Too Young

Even though Ed was 80 years old, I don't mean to generalize. There are plenty of older people who are more than willing to experience things they've never done before. For example, former President George Bush *voluntarily* parachuted out of an airplane for the first time at age 72, and then again three years later.

But amazingly there are too many people, barely into their 20s, whose greatest fear is some disruption in the lives they've already carefully constructed for themselves.

There also are plenty of couples in their 30s whose relationships have soured. And many times they are only too willing to throw those relationships away—unwilling to adapt to an evolving partner who could offer them the opportunity to *grow* with them.

And for many of those in their 40s, whose jobs have turned into drudgery, adapting to a new environment, a calling, an opportunity, or way of performing simply isn't considered an option.

And too many people in their 50s and 60s, facing the prospect of change from retirement or biology, refuse to greet the challenge and manage the inevitable.

People of every age, at any time, choose not to expand on their ability to adapt. They surrender new experiences in favor of routine. Excitement slips away from them in favor of familiar steps. They prefer sameness of everything and everyone, rather than the variety and diversity available to them—and complain at the same time that they're bored. And the opportunities they are given which would enable them to achieve so much more in life simply evaporate, many times going unnoticed.

Now think of someone or some organization that's lost its ability to adapt. If you can think of an example that involves you directly, use it. Consider as many details as you can about how the ability to accommodate a new situation began to slip away. And, if you can, think of specific episodes that document the slide—how it affected people, relationships, and causes. If it involved you directly, think of the relationships you lost, or didn't gain, as a result of your unwillingness to adapt.

Now consider how your perspective has changed—if it has. Sometimes the world unfolds largely without us and we may be left clinging to causes that no longer make a difference. Or we may ignore new developments that could change our lives for the better if we'd only acknowledge and embrace them.

If you have some question about whether or not you need to recapture or fine-tune your ability to adapt, do this simple review. Look for examples of the phrases "I can't" and "I won't" in your conversations. The perspectives reflected in these words will give you some insight into where you are willing to venture, and where you may have decided you'll no longer go. You may have been using these limiting statements for a long time without ever noticing them.

Of course, "I can't" may be linked to some physical or emotional challenge that literally won't allow you to engage the people or pursue the goals you once did. Too often, though, "I can't" is confused with "I won't"—the conscious, almost militant decision to stand your ground no matter what.

Just think about this. Anyone using "I can't" is generally taking the stance of a victim. People who do so often may figure, "How can anyone disagree with me if I say that I can't do something?" They don't even realize they have given away their power to make a positive decision and to take action to better their situation. And it's this mind-set that can keep anyone where they are, afraid to even consider living the life that holds fulfillment and rewards.

In Theresa's case, "I can't" held her at the side of the pool until she decided that, in fact, she *could.*

As for Ed, "I won't" never changed. Of course he could taste the new fruit. It was his choice not to. Sadly, he decided his days of adapting and enjoying new experiences were over. Directing the journey for the rest of his life simply never occurred to him.

Just realize that you *do* have the power to change in virtually every area of your life. It's up to you to say *"I can"* and go do it. It's simply a positive, proactive choice.

Chapter 15

Exercise Your Power to Choose
Claim Your Victory Over "Fate"

*"You always have a choice. People can
confuse themselves about directing their lives
because they sometimes opt out—choose not to choose.
Then they may wonder why they're
not getting what they want."*
Michael Kerrigan

It's a popular misconception that there are times when you don't
have a choice. It may have to do with accepting a job, entering a
relationship, building your own independent business, or deter-
mining some other course in life to take.

The truth is you *always* have a choice. People can confuse
themselves about directing their lives because they sometimes
opt out—they choose *not* to choose. Then they may wonder
why they're not getting what they want. They stay stuck on the
track they've be on for years, regardless of how unproductive
or damaging it may be. They may complain about it, but they
don't *do* anything about it. That *is* a choice. And don't be
fooled into thinking that it isn't.

Have you ever told yourself, "I'll just pass on this one. I simply won't choose." And what was the outcome? Didn't you just
let someone else choose for you?

You may think that by not choosing, you don't have to accept the
consequences. By not choosing, you may believe you have removed
yourself from the equation. But, of course, you haven't.

When you *don't* choose, you get what randomly comes your way.
In some cases, that may be okay. Fate may smile on you and say,
"Here, I'll give you one." But don't count on it.

Sure, a stock that shows every sign of losing ground in the market may maintain its value, or even buck a trend and shoot up. Or a former best friend or partner who's been drifting away reverses his or her trend and comes back into your life, more committed than ever to your relationship. Or the job you've held for so long—that's been targeted for downsizing—is transferred to another division and spared the budget axe.

Yes, miracles have been known to happen. In the vast majority of cases, though, fate isn't nearly so kind, especially when you choose not to act. You may end up with the rejects or leftovers of someone who *did* choose—someone who *did* exert self-responsibility. Who knows! You could be left with failed stock, a dissolved relationship, a cut in pay, or the loss of your job. These things happen. But they don't have to stop you. It all depends on the choices you make.

Remember. *When you choose, you influence outcomes!*

Naturally, there will always be unforeseen consequences, regardless of how active a role you may play. But consequences are always easier to handle when you participate in the process and make yourself heard.

Exerting your power of influence toward achieving whatever outcome you want is a direct result of choosing a goal. And the key in getting goal-setting to work for you is to support your goal with smaller, ongoing choices. Successful people use this process all the time—because it works!

One Step at a Time

Imagine anyone who climbs to the presidency of the United States or becomes an explorer, a business leader, an artist, or something else that requires focus and effort without consciously saying, *"This is what I want!"* It's tough to imagine, because it just doesn't work like that.

Even those who don't aspire to public office, or power, or uniqueness, but who are successful in their own right, make the conscious choice to succeed. It's a big choice and it sets the course for their lives. That big, self-directing move lies at the heart of going to college, getting married, accepting a job, building a business, making a big investment, retiring, and many other significant life decisions.

Fortunately, you don't need to make these big choices every day. What to do with your life is a decision that you're faced with only occasionally. And you usually only discover the road you are to take after careful consideration of your true wants, and conversations with those who support you in reaching your potential.

Once you've identified your goal, it's time to put all the little choices to work. These supporting choices are an active, ongoing part of life. And addressing them is just as important as pursuing your big choices, because the small choices are the stepping stones to your goal.

Matt's case illustrates how his small choices supported his big choice and helped him reach his goal. After pondering his options, he decided to apply to the U.S. Air Force Academy. This was his big choice—making the commitment to go. And it wasn't made lightly.

Matt had already attended college for a year. But in the academy's eyes that didn't count. The Air Force has its own academic system, meaning Matt would have to start at the beginning, once again.

The highly regimented life at the academy was another issue Matt considered in making his big choice. He would face four years of a rigid structure and a battery of tough technical courses. The free-thinking ways of a public university and civilian life would have to be left far behind.

Next, Matt also needed to consider the five years he'd have to spend after graduation as a commissioned officer. Four years at the academy, followed by five years of active duty made for a nine-year commitment. Matt would then be 28.

The big choice of affiliating with the Air Force would affect how others related to him, as well as how Matt viewed himself. No doubt, a whole line of additional career choices will be his based on his education and years in the service. And in all likelihood, these choices wouldn't be available to him if he hadn't selected the Academy. They would be part of his reward.

I've laid out the elements of Matt's big choice. The small choices he needs to make to support his decision—and succeed— will be ongoing.

He'll have to persevere through the first month of basic training and the hazing heaped on each incoming freshman. The small choices of saluting and obeying the orders of everyone with whom he would come in contact will have to become automatic. Studying under extreme conditions, eating in calculated silence, and severing nearly all contact with the outside world—all these things entered into Matt's choice-making process.

Matt's had to make plenty of choices, and there will be many more to come. He could have chosen not to apply to the Academy in the first place. And when he was accepted, he could have chosen not to go. He could choose not to salute, or study, or observe the strict rules of his new environment. But a non-choice, in essence a negative choice, would only defeat his goal of the education and career he's told himself he wants.

Just like Matt, you too have many choices. The first thing required to make any change you want to make is that you need to—*exercise your option to choose.*

Going Out of Your Own Way

Think of the last time you said to yourself, "I want that," or, "I want to express myself to him or her." With that goal in mind:

- What did you need to do to get what you wanted?
- How did you need to change your behavior, at least temporarily?
- What sacrifices did you make that you never would have thought were necessary, or even reasonable?
- What changes in behavior did you need to make?
- Which choices worked for you, and which didn't?

Whether you were changing your behavior or making sacrifices, you were making choices. You may not have been aware of the process while you were in the middle of it, but the process was happening just the same. How much control you exerted during the process was up to you.

The next time you're given a choice, think of the steps you took to make your previous goal a success. Considering each step will help you put your new goal into a truer perspective.

Remember to use all the tools—the choices, analysis, reason, and support—available to you when you decide to reach for your goal.

Chapter 16

Are You Living a Puppet's Life?
If So, Cut the Strings and Choose Your Destiny

"You can *choose your own destiny, and you*
need the approval of only one person to get started.
That person is you!*"*
Michael Kerrigan

Take a minute and think back to when you were a kid. You're rummaging around in your toy box and there, asleep in the corner, is a hand puppet.

You snatch him from the box, shove your tiny hand up his back, and make him start spouting the words only you are thinking. The conversation is of your choosing, as you jump from one topic to the next. You and your puppet are as perfectly synchronized as a team of Olympic skaters.

But the real beauty of this character perched at the end of your arm is that he has no thoughts of his own. He doesn't contradict what you believe. He speaks only when you want him to. And when you grow tired of him, he quietly goes back into the box and waits without complaint until you pick him up again to give him life. It's a nice arrangement—if you happen to be the puppet master. But it's a bleak existence if you're the puppet.

Fortunately the puppet doesn't have to anguish about his situation. The puppet doesn't worry about the years slipping by in service to someone who resurrects him from the box only when he wants to.

Have *you* ever felt like a puppet? Unfortunately, there are way too many opportunities to fill that role. They flourish in nearly every setting where people interact, whether it's in business, at school, or with personal relationships.

For example, consider a highly structured organization with a strong, dominant leader. Just below him or her you're likely to find a layer of vice presidents who compliment their boss's every utterance, and whose standard reply is *yes*. For all practical purposes they are puppets with no thoughts of their own, or at least no thoughts they're willing to share with the person who controls them. There's too much risk.

At each vice president's immediate command is a layer of directors and division managers, who largely fill the same function of unwavering support. In their puppet roles, they tell the vice presidents only what they want to hear.

Below the directors are the middle managers, staffers, and technicians, who play their own supportive roles. Experience has told these subordinates that dissent leads to isolation. And those who are isolated – who don't function as team players – are easy targets for firing.

In an organization that operates with rigid rules, from top to bottom, the voice of honest discussion—let alone of differing values—is rarely heard. Those presumably hired for their intelligence and abilities basically become nothing more than followers.

And the repercussions for these potential producers can be devastating. Rather than contributing to the organization's goals, well-being, and success, followers are often ignored. Resentment is a likely result. Any cohesion that may have existed often evaporates, and an organization can fall to pieces.

Under these circumstances, feelings of frustration and rage can be buried beneath rigid, humorless lives. Another part of the fallout could even result in alcohol and drug abuse. It's part of a scenario of believing you need to suppress who you are or what you're thinking. And the feelings of isolation can be overwhelming and potentially devastating.

Let Me In

Even under the worst circumstances, few people choose to surrender themselves entirely just to get along. But that doesn't mean people don't give up a piece of themselves every day just to fit into some structure.

We're social creatures. For the most part, we work in groups. Even those who work by themselves ultimately plug their projects or study results into a group.

We join places of worship, networking groups, and clubs. We see movies and plays and go to business conventions and sports events of huge crowds. Even if we rent a video or watch a football game alone, we seek out others who have also seen the dramatic scene or game-winning play to talk about it.

Socialization is well ingrained. It starts when we're children, often with mom seeking out playmates for us. Relationships with other kids follow and continue through elementary school, scouts, sports teams, and clubs.

As adults, we sign up for leagues, join associations, take out memberships, volunteer, get second jobs, build businesses, and learn to line dance. And while these ventures give us knowledge and skills, they also provide contact with other people.

When you're not connected, you're alone, and most people will do almost anything to escape such a fate. They're often frightened by the prospect of going to a movie, out to dinner, or heading home by themselves.

Most of us strive to belong to the best group we can. But the price can be high. Too often, the process demands that we sacrifice some part of who we are, whether that sacrifice is time, dignity, beliefs, or convictions.

The Price of Admission

Now let's examine all sides of something you're involved in by asking yourself several questions. It could be your job, a social club, community involvement, or some other commitment. And if you want to, you could also apply this to a long-term relationship. The question is, what did you give up to join or commit to it?

We all make sacrifices when it comes to making choices and accommodating change, and that can be okay. No situation, organization, or person can offer us *everything*. And that's what you need to look at now. Are you giving up too much of yourself in order to belong? Remember that surrendering too much of who you are can render you little more than a puppet.

Now look at the same question from the other side. What did you *gain* by joining that organization or entering into that relationship? What good did it do you?

Sacrifice is normal, and most of us are willing to give up something for something else of greater return—a more productive business relationship, a more challenging and rewarding job, or a more interesting group of friends. Giving up doesn't have to be a negative thing. It's simply part of growing and moving on.

A Quick Look *Back*

If you've lost perspective on the process of change, go to your old storage boxes or trunk (you might even find that hand puppet still there) and get out the family photo album. Open it up and take a look at the pictures. What you'll see is undeniable evidence of change. From baby pictures to photos of broad grins with missing teeth, from first cars and first dates, to graduation and first apartments. This is a visual reminder of change, and much of it is positive. Now continue on through the photos of vacations, friends, weddings, and pictures of your kids.

The physical changes we undergo, documented in these photos, are a tribute to our ability to grow, adapt, and mature. The process is normal and natural and—finally—inevitable. Some of us go to great lengths trying to escape, or at least cushion the impact from those mounting years. The tools to soften these physical changes range from plastic surgery and lying about our age, to a mad dash into jogging, aerobics, racquetball, and rock climbing.

While the physical changes we undergo can be documented in photographs, the mental changes we experience aren't nearly as clean and obvious. While personal maturity can develop just as freely as aging, psychological change requires one big thing that *physical change* brought about by aging doesn't—our permission.

You *can* choose your own destiny, and you need the approval of only one person to get started. And that person is *you!* It's a key step if you are going to live a life that is full and rewarding. And it's absolutely essential if you are going to escape the world of the puppets.

Chapter 17

How to Negotiate a Win
Reach Agreements That Benefit Everyone

"Principled behavior
is the cornerstone of Win/Win.
It establishes your character. And you demonstrate the
quality of your character every day
through your actions."
Michael Kerrigan

We all make deals. We make them with bosses, clients, business associates, spouses, kids—the works. And while each one is different, the process leading up to it is the same. It's the negotiation.

Now think about the last time you negotiated something—anything. It could have been business-related, or a negotiation with the next-door neighbor about the height of the fence around her yard. Or it may have been a discussion and agreement with your son about chores and allowance.

Look back to that negotiation, then answer this question: *What was your frame of mind during your discussions?*

Were you out for everything you could get? Or were you determined to reach a fair, mutually beneficial agreement that everyone involved would be happy about?

Your frame of mind has everything to do with your establishing quality relationships. Because the attitude that drives the discussions that lead to agreements will define those agreements forever. You'll be remembered for how you conducted yourself and how you treated your counterpart during the negotiation.

If it's a positive experience, the deal's likely to produce a solid working relationship. But if a deal's struck and there's a lingering doubt about its fairness, that cloud will affect how business is conducted both under that agreement and under any future agreements you may have with that person.

Such a Deal

Take the case of Will. He ran the communications department at Call Back Incorporated. Call Back's reputation was great within the community. This corporation was seen as a leader in the industry. People working in other related businesses often imagined themselves jumping to Call Back, if given half a chance.

Openings in Will's department were almost unheard of. Recently, though, a job did open up. The salary range spanned more than $20,000, from low to high—depending on the applicant's experience.

Will received more than 300 applications for the job. To give you some sense of Call Back's desirability as an employer, 12 of those applications were from attorneys—even though the job had nothing to do with law!

After a lengthy interview process, Will hired Carl who had extraordinary experience working for 15 years as an editor, researcher, and commentator. The two of them got along from the minute they met. Carl's strengths complemented the abilities of other staff members. He was just the person Will had dreamed of hiring.

When it came to the salary, though, Will offered Carl the lowest possible. Carl wanted the job, which gave Will the upper hand. Will reasoned that it was a seller's market. He was firm in the salary offer. Will said he couldn't offer Carl anything more.

As it turned out, the high end of the advertised salary was nothing more than a hook to get people interested. Will had no intention of paying that much, even though Call Back could easily have afforded the maximum.

Despite his disappointment, and after several attempts to get Will to increase the salary, Carl took the job. And he resented Will every day he came into work. What looked like a promising, cooperative relationship never materialized. It never even came close.

Will saw Carl as weak, no different than anyone else who just needed a job. Carl saw Will as someone who would say *anything* to get what he wanted. Carl never linked Will and honesty in the same thought.

Will's frame of mind, even before his negotiations with Carl began, was skewed. It was skewed toward winning at the least expense to the corporation, no matter what credentials an applicant brought to the table. Therefore, Carl—or anyone taking the job—would be on the losing end. For the most part, Will *was* in control, especially of the purse strings. Of course, Carl shares some of the burden. He *could* have refused the job.

But let's back up to the point where Will began the interview with Carl. The two of them got along fine from the instant they met. Will could see that Carl's abilities would compensate for the weaknesses of other staff members. Carl was just the person Will had dreamed of hiring. So why in the world did their negotiation take the course that it did?

It's the Principle

This is where three important components enter the equation—*principles, character, and self-interest.*

Let's evaluate each component, as they all touch on some element of the negotiation and the frame of mind that went with it.

First, let's look at Will's principles—his ethical standards:

- How ethical was Will in the way he handled Carl and the salary offer?
- How obliged was Will to give Carl more than the minimum advertised salary?
- Was Carl right to have expected more because of his experience and the contribution he was being asked to make— bringing along his own unique talents as well as making up for staff deficiencies?

Now look at Will's character:

- What moral obligation, if any, was Will under to offer Carl more money?
- Was there anything wrong with the take-it-or-leave-it position Will adopted and Carl accepted?

Finally, consider the issue of Will's self-interest:

- What, if anything, was wrong with Will coming out on top in the negotiation?
- Will's a competitive guy, and he's been that way all his life. As far as he's concerned, he won and Carl lost. It happens every day. What, if anything, is wrong with this perspective?
- How could the overall situation have been improved, or could it?
- Is there a scenario in which both Will and Carl could have felt like they had both emerged as winners?

Principled behavior is the cornerstone of win/win. It establishes your character. And you demonstrate the quality of your character every day through your choices and actions.

The challenging thing about this public display of who you are could be that everyone's watching, from absolute strangers to those with whom you have the most intimate relationships. Each one of these people is able to assess your character from their own perspective simply by watching and listening to you.

And they'll decide in an instant whether or not you're relationship material. Strangers will take the next step to get to know you better, or turn and walk away without saying a word. While those you already share some part of your life with will probably hang in there with you, others who have more or less contact with you may cast you aside altogether.

If this sounds a little raw, it is. It's also a fact. People make choices about relationships all the time. It's a process that never ends. And these choices lead to a second date or a cold shoulder, a new hire or a firing, a new client or customer, a missed opportunity, or another term in elected office or an unexpected defeat. And while no particular outcome is absolutely assured when it comes to dealing with other people, you can definitely influence it by your character.

It's Your Call

Now, most of us want our encounters to be positive when we make the effort to relate to others. Who in his or her right mind would want to behave in a way that would alienate someone else? (Okay, the operative phrase here is *right mind*.)

It's true that some people just don't get it when it comes to compassion or civility. They go through a daily routine that virtually offends everybody. If a relationship actually develops with someone else, it's probably out of the other person's necessity or desperation. A trusting, productive relationship isn't likely to happen. Others will simply evaluate anyone who acts like a jerk and decide they don't want anything to do with him or her. They've got enough challenges as it is, and don't want more. They can see "the writing on the wall."

But you don't always have the option of walking away from someone whose behavior is boorish, overbearing, or just plain rude—especially if you work for someone else. To this degree, work relationships are a lot like those with relatives—you don't get to pick them. For the most part, you probably don't get to choose who you work with.

And this is where your *willingness, ability, and action* again come into play. Earlier, we looked at the role these three elements have in establishing new relationships. In an earlier case, Lyle showed that he was willing and had the ability to effectively relate to others. He was a natural. It was simply his failure to act that stood in the way of his creating new relationships. He never took that first step to achieve what he *said* he wanted.

And it's exactly at this point that a lot of people lose their momentum to establish effective connections with others. They meet someone whom they would like to contact for business or other purposes but they're afraid of being rejected. Taking action can be both frightening and exciting, especially the positive action that enables someone else to experience victory along with you. It allows someone to get to know the real you, and there's more at stake.

Letting others get close enough to see who you really are can seem threatening. To a large degree, it means letting down your guard—the one you may have built up to keep from getting hurt. When you're open and vulnerable, you can certainly experience negative consequences. That's true for all of us.

But remember, all sorts of *positive* experiences can occur as well. For these to happen, though, you need to make sure you are paying attention to what's going on around you, who you are interacting with, how you are treating them, and your goals for the encounter. This last point may sound a little calculating, but it's not meant to take advantage of the other person. It's not like Will's attitude toward Carl, who both appeared earlier in this chapter.

Establishing mutually advantageous goals for a relationship allows everyone involved to make the most of it. And paying attention to what the other person is saying is a compliment to them. It tells him or her that you are interested and concerned. It also helps you determine if you're focusing properly and using your time to its fullest.

The Hurdles to Reaching Agreements

When it comes to win/win, there are two primary elements that can get in the way: *self-interest* and *factionalism*.

It's true we all want what's best for ourselves. We are *self-interested*. It's just human nature. We all seek out comfort, stability, happiness—the list goes on and on. We focus on ourselves. Us. And the typical question we have is, "What's in it for me?"

Others, especially those outside our immediate family, may come in a distant second—if their needs are considered at all, particularly when what they want conflicts with *our* needs. That's why people who go into religious work are viewed as so exceptional. They put others first on a regular basis. The fact is that doing this is what makes them feel good about themselves—they're making a difference. And as pure and enviable as that might appear to be, most of the rest of us simply don't bother.

Ask the majority of people to give a little, or to surrender some part of what they have, and they'll look at you like you've escaped from an asylum or are speaking gibberish. Once the focus is taken away from *their* wants and needs, their interest quickly vanishes. On a larger scale, this emphasis on "Who's getting what?" is called *factionalism*.

It's normal to bond with those who look at the world the same way that you do. Join up with a couple of like-minded individuals and you've got a faction. Add a few more and these alliances can turn into labor unions, political parties, places of worship, associations, organizations, and other entities. Like-minded people coming together to achieve a common goal is a normal turn of events.

Negotiation—*The Missing Link*

But how often is bargaining part of a faction's mind-set?

How frequently, instead, is confrontation used as a tool to get what the faction wants from someone or another group? In a lot of cases, members of a faction look around and figure that the numbers are on their side. But even as a member of a faction, you can't control everything.

How much easier would it be if give-and-take discussions were part of the everyday dialogue with others outside the group? Naturally, that would require negotiation and compromise. And it also means that those with other, possibly conflicting goals got some of what *they* need.

Effective communication is usually the first element thrown out the window when self-interest and factionalism come into play. Look at any business or organization experiencing internal challenges and you're likely to find that reasoned communication just doesn't exist. Productive discussions are often replaced by silence, orders, and threats. What's missing is *listening*. And active, empathetic listening is one of the most effective agents for establishing a win/win scenario among those whose primary interest is self-centered.

Unless you find common ground for discussion, first by truly listening, hearing, and understanding what the other person has said, and then making yourself clear in a nonthreatening way, you're not going to get your point across. Civil, goal-oriented talks provide the most streamlined way of creating a win/win situation and making it work for you.

The alternative to win/win is standing in opposing corners, unwilling to compromise, only meeting halfway in order to fight. That doesn't sound like much fun, now does it?

Keeping an Open Mind

Now let's explore your own negotiating style by dividing it into two parts.

First, consider the last *successful* negotiation you had by answering these questions:

- What was the issue?
- Was the discussion pursued by you, or the person you negotiated with?
- How was the issue brought up?

- What were the circumstances?
- Was confrontation involved?
- Was the negotiation conducted in a logical, orderly way?
- How long did it take to negotiate an agreement?
- What elements were involved that allowed a positive outcome—trust, understanding, patience, dedication to reaching a successful agreement?

Second, consider the last negotiation you had that *failed* by answering these questions:

- What kept that negotiation from being successful?
- Was it because of some technical hang-up, or did pride and personalities torpedo any hope of an agreement?
- What could have led to a successful outcome?
- What might you have done differently to reach an agreement?
- And what compromise could the person you were negotiating with have made to make a deal happen?

Don't let your old ways, or anything else for that matter, get in the way of the issue. Focus on coming up with a solution that benefits both parties.

Remember, the person you're sitting across the table from or talking with on the phone is a human being just like you. His or her feelings probably aren't much different than yours. So it only makes sense that he or she will respond more positively to a constructive atmosphere and words of respect. And it's almost guaranteed that their position will harden when an attack is launched on their reputation or company, or the way they part their hair.

Just remember to keep your focus on *what* you're negotiating rather than who you're negotiating with.

People frequently get stuck in habits and ruts that don't allow them to think in creative ways. Don't let this happen to you. The next time you negotiate anything, think in broader terms where the other person's wants and needs become part of the solution. When you do, the alternatives available to you will be much greater than you could ever have imagined. You might even find room for a decision that satisfies everyone, and the challenge of win/win will be met.

Chapter 18

Learn to Link Freedom and Choice
The Decision Is Yours to Make

*"People who win determine their
own course with each decision they make and action
they take—minute-by-minute, hour-by-hour, day-by-day.
They take personal responsibility for their own lives and then act.
It's their choice and they know it."*
Michael Kerrigan

The opportunity to make quality choices is with you every minute of every day. Your choices include what time you get out of bed, how you treat your family, associates, coworkers, and others, what you do with your money, how you spend your free time, and where you worship.

It's all a matter of choice. But not everyone makes the best choices. Not everyone even believes that the choice is his or hers to make.

Take the case of Glenda, a partner in a medium-sized law firm. By her own admission, she's a fighter. "I used to fight on every point," she concedes, recalling her early days in the profession. "I wouldn't compromise. I believed that the lawyers with the best reputations were the toughest ones to deal with."

After ten years in the business, Glenda has tempered her behavior, at least a little. But she readily admits she's a tyrant. "You have to be," she concludes. "There's no choice if you're going to succeed."

But there's *always* a choice. It's called free will. And failure to exercise your free will is just one of the barriers you could create to frustrate yourself and stop your efforts in reaching new goals.

In choosing to fight every point Glenda alienated coworkers, adversaries, even some clients, as she went about the business of practicing law. She believed that even considering another approach was a sign of weakness.

But there are other less-dramatic, nondestructive ways for Glenda to score victories for her clients than screaming and intimidation. Diplomacy, the reading of the law, even flawless preparation are just some of the options. They all provide different paths leading to the same goal of winning.

Free will and choices have been around forever, and they are absolutely indispensable for anyone who wants to live the most effective life possible.

Now, you may not believe you're free to act in the most rewarding way you can. You may be thinking, "I'm stuck. I'm in a job I can't leave. I have financial commitments I can't abandon. I have a reputation to maintain. There are no choices."

Regardless of what you may tell yourself, and despite your own programs that tell you there is only one way to act, remember this—*you always have a choice to do what's best for you.* And all you need to do is exercise your free will to make it happen.

A Sure Thing

Some people manage to keep themselves locked in place—never attempting anything new—by convincing themselves they're born to lose. That "Born to Lose" motto, that scarred the arms of motorcycle gangs across America in the 1960s, simply isn't true. No one is *born* to lose.

Imagine for a minute a newborn who's internally programmed to end up drunk in a gutter 30 years in the future. Regardless of genetic encoding and half-a-dozen other medical and psychological theories, this child isn't predestined to simply trade in a bottle of formula for a bottle of liquor.

Despite the dueling theories of nurture vs. nature, any one of us can turn his or her life around regardless of the circumstances, as challenging as that may appear to be. People do it all the time. There are people raised by a family of drinkers who turn their backs on alcohol. Individuals who were raised in atmospheres of poverty and neglect find jobs, build businesses, and raise productive families.

People who win determine their own course with each decision they make and action they take—minute by minute, hour by hour, day by day. They take personal responsibility for their own lives, and then act. It's their choice and they know it. They choose to win and then follow through to make it happen, doing even the uncomfortable things they need to do.

This isn't to say that their personal programs may not be stacked against them. The messages they received from parents and others telling them they were no good or will never amount to anything may be very real. But being born to lose is hard, if not impossible, to accept—even for those of us deeply entrenched in negative programming.

Consider the different paths of Mac and Andy.

Mac was a brilliant kid. He excelled in all aspects of school, from math and science to languages. And he was popular for his funny, occasionally outrageous behavior. Born into an upper-middle class family, Mac could have done anything. Gone to any college. Selected any profession. It was his choice. He opted for a local college, where he struggled for a year before dropping out. Ten years after leaving school, he managed to reenter and got a degree in business.

The drugs and alcohol he'd taken during that lost decade had little impact on his quick wit. After graduation, he made a half-hearted attempt at being in business. But, as was his habit, he never really committed to it and quit after making a meager effort. Today, Mac is living on society's fringes, jumping from one menial job to the next, with no vision of what next month will bring, let alone next year.

And then there's Andy. Andy had a lot of obstacles, right from the beginning. His parents divorced when he was still in grade school. His mother remarried and the family moved away from their support network of relatives and friends. The kids were largely responsible for raising themselves.

Andy could be menacing, but he typically wore a disarming smile. He excelled in athletics and rode that success until the demands of sports finally exceeded his abilities. He then shifted his energies to studying and working hard to carry himself through college and earn a degree. Today, he's a successful journalist.

Andy could have collapsed at any one of several points during his life. He could have thrown his hands up and walked away from his future, blaming his past for the outcome. People could have said he was born to lose. But Andy didn't make excuses and walk away. Instead, *he chose* to succeed.

Mac, on the other hand, was born to win, or so it would seem. But by any reasonable standard, he didn't. At each step in his life, Mac chose. He chose against discipline. He chose against his potential. He chose what was comfortable and lived in the survival zone.

At birth your potential is unlimited. And so are your choices to achieve that promise. Making smart, basic choices will help you as you move toward identifying your goals and make the necessary positive changes so you can accomplish them one by one.

Fight Any Urge to Self-Destruct

Some percentage of people inadvertently choose to self-destruct before they ever get a chance to exercise their free will.

Some of you may remember the opening scene from the 1960s television show *Mission Impossible.* The suave, blond Jim steps into a telephone booth to take the week's impossible assignment from a tape recording. At the end of the instructions, and the obligatory *good luck* from the mysterious voice, the tape self-destructs. With a flash of chemical smoke, it evaporates.

So it is with many of us. We self-destruct. Unfortunately, we don't have the privacy of a telephone booth to commit our acts of personal sabotage. Usually they're performed in public. But unlike the tape, our self-destruction isn't in the name of national security— nothing so glamorous.

Self-destruction keeps us from growing in personal and professional relationships. It keeps us frozen where we are, frustrated with life, fighting ourselves over things that would never have become issues if we had made positive choices and taken appropriate action on them.

One basic form of self-destruction is ignoring responsibilities. You've seen it before. The needle next to the little gas tank on your car's dashboard is sitting next to empty. "Lucky I saw that," you say to yourself. And you keep driving—to the grocery store, to pick up the kids, to drop off the laundry.

You may pass up opportunity after opportunity to fill up the tank, while the situation becomes more and more threatening and you finally coast to a stop at the side of the road. Even the gasoline fumes have evaporated. And you're left calling for help, or trudging to the nearest gas station for a gallon of unleaded.

Repairing the damage you inflict on yourself—or others—is ten times more difficult than it would be to simply act responsibly in the first place!

Of course, you may have never run out of gas. Any self-destructive behavior you may have may be more subtle. You could have made some inappropriate comment, failed to acknowledge someone, or ignored some act of kindness. Then, the instant after the misdeed takes place, you generally know it's wrong. To make matters worse, you fail to apologize and correct the problem. And the moment floats by carrying the offense with it, only to be replaced by self-inflicted anger, or embarrassment, or some other feeling screaming at you from inside for your inadequacy.

Unfortunately, that becomes your legacy. That moment and that behavior is how those involved remember you. It provides the basis of how others expect you to act in the future. And you may well anticipate the same thing of yourself. It can serve as the model for your future behavior, unless you let go of it and take steps to change.

Knowing how to identify any unreasonable, unacceptable behavior you may have is the first step toward correcting it.

Walk the Talk

The final hurdle that may be standing in the way of exercising your free will is negative self-talk.

Now while talking to yourself isn't generally considered a sign of insanity, in some cases it could be. People chattering away to no one in particular on the street corner may not have it all together. But these people, babbling strings of words at the trees and buildings, are the exception.

We all talk to ourselves—sometimes a word at a time, sometimes with canned phrases or in complete sentences. You may do it silently, in a voice barely exceeding a whisper, or completely out loud. You could encourage yourself to make a sale or an association, rehash a conversation you had from the night before, or berate yourself for having made a mistake.

It's this last example that's all too common—the negative self-talk we use to punish ourselves. And it's everywhere.

Look at Cal. He's an intelligent high school administrator in his mid-40s. The father of two grown, successful sons, Cal is engaging to his peers and a prized resource for the students he deals with daily. And like everyone else, Cal makes an occasional mistake. But rather than quickly examining why things have gone wrong and correcting the error, Cal scolds himself with the word "Stupid!"

Things just erupt and go completely out of character. Cal then moves on, never consciously considering the self-defeating blast he just gave himself. On its face, the comment seems incidental. But ask him if he thinks he's stupid and he'll tell you, "Of course not." Nevertheless, it *is* part of his self-talk—an habitual part of his mental program. And it's negative.

The real obstacle comes when Cal is confronted by some challenging situation, one that requires him to think, perform, or come up with a creative solution. And when he taps his mental program, doing a quick search of his resources for an answer, Cal runs into "Stupid!" He can let that program lock him in place, unable to provide a solution to a situation he *can* handle.

Could *you* come up with a great solution if your programming tells you you're stupid, or gives you one of a dozen other twisted messages that stand in the way of achieving your goals? Probably not. Begin replacing any negative self-talk you may have had with words of encouragement and success. Give yourself the best choice you can, and a chance to change for the better.

The following choices are available to you every day. They can help you in every way imaginable, when you exercise your will to choose:

- Build on your strengths and follow your dream. Choose an opportunity that can enable you to make it come true, and ask for help from those who are where *you* want to be.
- Believe in yourself. When you're truly challenged, you are the best, most reliable resource you have.

- Accept others as they are. But see them as they can be, and support them in reaching their potential. Search out those with whom you can compatibly work and accomplish win/win outcomes.
- Decide for yourself. Effective choice-making for yourself leads to personal empowerment.
- Take responsibility for all your actions. Responsible choices are more likely to lead to effective outcomes.
- Work for what you believe in. A life lived with conviction is a life fulfilled.
- Heighten your awareness of every action you take. Learn from your mistakes.
- Involve yourself in every detail of your life. All that's required to start on a more beneficial road in any aspect of your life is your decision and the determination to make something positive happen. Then follow through with appropriate action. You can make it happen.

Chapter 19

You *Can* Pay the Price of Success
Or You *Will* Pay the Price of Failure

*"The old you is a thing of the past. Swept away, too,
is all of your emotional baggage, ineffective behaviors,
and repeated mistakes."*
Michael Kerrigan

There's no question that taking on new challenges and reaching higher goals will stir emotions you never anticipated—and may never have even wanted. But this is normal. Keep moving forward anyway.

Establishing new attitudes and behaviors *will* require you to establish priorities, focus on goals, and assert yourself in meaningful, productive ways. And as fulfilling and gratifying as this may be for you, it won't always be popular with others. It may not even be popular with the *old* you.

At this point, you need to make a choice to either take a new road or stay where you are. When you're committed to changing the way you behave and redefining what is important to you, you'll need to make some adjustments. This may include leaving behind some of the people you may like the most, including who you are *now*. And this is where the challenge may arise. For some, the loss can be so great that it may be like experiencing a death.

Imagine you're at a funeral. Among those sitting in the chapel and grieving the death is your family. All of your friends are also there. People from where you work, along with your most valued associates and clients, are all waiting in stunned silence for the service to begin.

Rather than joining them in the pews to pay your last respects, though, you are the one being mourned. You are the one lying in the casket, fitted in that navy blue suit you just got back from the cleaners. And you look terrific. But there's no doubt about it—*you've definitely passed on.*

The old you is now just a memory of the past. Swept away, too, is all of your emotional baggage—the fears, prejudices, ineffective behaviors, and repeated mistakes.

The saving grace about this little church drama, obviously, is that you're *not* gone. What you've just experienced in this funeral scene is the purging of your old self. What you have to look forward to is getting on with who you want to be—*from now on!*

Not So Fast

The funeral—mourning the loss of the old ways—is your farewell to the ineffective behavior that you allowed to hold you in place. And while *you* may be relieved, some people clearly won't be. They're likely to confront you with closed minds and bad reasoning to keep you from moving on. This is also normal.

There are two hurdles to overcome for the *new* you to fully emerge.

First, you need to say *bye-bye* to the old you. This is critical. Because once you've redefined who you are, giving old responses to new opportunities just won't work. As much as the old you may want to hang around, he or she has nothing more to contribute.

The second hurdle is managing and overcoming your grieving friends, relatives, and others who only know you as you *were*. And this grieving can take a while. The challenge is to deal effectively with those who only feel comfortable seeing you as a person frozen in time, a reliable person offering predictable responses to *their* needs.

Imagine the impact the death of your old self could have on the survival zone of others—how this departure of the old you is likely to affect them. Do your best to assess it from their points of view. Picture how your family, friends, and business associates—who are comfortable with you in one well-defined context—will see you when you break free.

Now go back to the funeral scene and focus on the mourners. Think of the pandemonium that would spread through the chapel if those who were so sorry to see the old you go were told there was a chance to bring you back! They could reconstruct your life, with you just the way you *were.*

The pressure would be relentless from all quarters—parents, children, golfing buddies, and bridge partners—all clamoring to get you back to make *them* comfortable. Think of all the praying, singing, and joking—every technique this resourceful group could think of—to resurrect the *old* you.

Now you may think such a scene is pretty unlikely. On the contrary, it's very real. Since you're not dead, your change in behavior can be seen by others as something to be fixed or cured. Your new way of doing things is likely to be observed as nothing more than an aberration of the way you were.

"He's just a little delusional today," they may say. "A little rest and he'll be as good as new (the way he was, that is)." Get ready for this, because this is the way some people are likely to respond to the new you.

But when you're going to make a positive change—one that you want—and make it last, you need to be willing to let go of the people who may stand in your way. Or you need to be strong enough to face those who are resisting your change and explain to them that you're not coming back the way you were.

Some of these people will be able to adjust—although your relationship with them will probably be different. The payoff could be their accepting you for who you want to be.

All growth requires effort, but that's what produces success. And your own personal growth is one of the greatest benefits of giving yourself the life you want.

Chapter 20

Scale the Ladder of Change
Reach Your Potential by Focusing and Acting

*"You don't have to be the person
officially designated as a leader to make positive
contributions—in any situation. There are tremendous
opportunities to be effective at all levels. All it takes is
your active involvement to bring it about."*
Michael Kerrigan

When was the last time you were really challenged? When were you pushed physically or mentally to a limit you hadn't approached in years, if ever?

Your challenge may have been an Outward Bound excursion, where you were expected to survive on your own. You may have presented your product, service, or opportunity for the first time. Or you may have been asked to speak to a group of coworkers about a project you were developing.

What was your response when you discovered you'd be taking on this task? Were you fearful or excited about the opportunity to stretch? The moment you embarked on this challenge, were you shivering with nervous anticipation? Was that edgy response triggered by fear or excitement? Could you tell? If you were confused, don't be too surprised. The two reactions tap the same emotional core. The significant difference is that excitement will propel you into action, while fear will freeze you right where you are.

If your goal is positive change, you need to decide which emotion you're feeling and how you're going to deal with it. Remember—*you have a choice.*

Imagine that your challenge comes in the form of a ladder. The ladder's left side represents fear, while the right side represents *excitement!* If you approach the challenge steeped in fear, you're likely to clutch the left side and stay precisely where you are. Moving up the ladder just won't happen. Even getting close enough to it to analyze your challenge will be a struggle. But when you're excited about where you're headed, you'll grab the right side of the ladder and start reaching for one level after another. For most people, progress up the ladder begins somewhere in the middle of those two sides—between fear and excitement.

Establishing the *pivotal point* between fear and excitement, and dealing effectively with change is different for everyone. But it's essential that you identify that point, because finding it is the first step toward progressing toward your goal.

More than Simple Chaos

Once you commit to getting on the ladder of change, you will face four rungs: Chaos, Survival, Mission, and Effectiveness. The specifics of each are as unique as each person who occupies or climbs the ladder. Ideally, progressing from one rung to the next is the objective of choice.

Now consider a challenge virtually everyone can identify with—work. If you are employed, recall the first day of your current job. You were probably shown your desk or workspace, the lounge, the rest room, the copier, the supply closet, and a stack of state and federal forms awaiting your signature. You were then given a load of company regulations, policies and procedures, training manuals, and orientation schedules. The situation could have been overwhelming.

What you found on that first day of your job was *chaos*, even before you started the work you were hired to perform. And unless you ran screaming from the building, you successfully scaled the first rung of the ladder. You got the chaos under control and advanced to the second rung—*survival.*

But survival was a different animal. Here you were required to negotiate the pitfalls and promises of your new job. You needed to perform the related tasks, at least adequately. You discovered the power centers and identified the untouchable and the unspeakable. You met allies, as well as those who were working for their own interests *only*. You learned how not to get burned. You managed to survive. You mastered the second level and were ready to move on to the next rung.

But wait a minute. Unless you're exceptional, survival is probably where you stopped. This is where many people stall in their efforts to establish a new life. They learn how to survive, and survival is what they settle for. Around some offices they're known as *dead wood*. They're the marginal performers, just good enough to keep their jobs. Their mission is to retire. The fact that retirement may still be 20 years away makes little difference to them. Evolution just isn't in their vocabulary. Their life is so-so—same old, same old. Growth and maturity doesn't happen for them.

So what are the rewards for scaling the ladder past survival? How about a more fulfilling life, greater contacts, and a range of options that would never be available to you if you had just stayed where you were?

Now let's assume that *you* are moving on to the third rung—*mission*. It involves identifying why you live your life or, in this case, do your job or business most effectively. In essence, this is your purpose. Not only does it have a huge impact on you, but it also affects others as well.

Where you choose to live, the profession or business and pastimes you engage in, and the creed you believe in, not only affect you but have a direct impact on those around you. Figuring out your role on the ladder's third rung requires some serious thought, and not everyone is willing to do this. Not everyone is willing to push him or herself to the next level, where they can discover their true calling and realize their sense of maximum self-worth.

Let's focus on your job or business to gauge how effectively you are operating and determine where your opportunities lie:

- How do you fit in?
- Are you doing what's expected of you?
- Are you doing what you expect of yourself?
- How are you contributing to your own professional growth, or that of your business?

- How can you grow beyond the expectations of those you work with *and* for?
- And what initiative have you taken to make yourself more valuable to yourself and your organization?

The Mission step is an integral part of scaling the ladder, and it's one you need to take before reaching the ladder's top rung—*effectiveness*. And effectiveness is about leadership.

To fulfill the effectiveness rung you need to interact with conviction, desire, and honesty. Whether that's on the job or in your business, within your family, at your place of worship, organization, or somewhere else, effectiveness means advancing the cause and achieving *more* for the benefit of all concerned.

Climbing and Falling

I once worked on a rural daily newspaper, with a small but extremely talented staff. During my first year there, the paper won a huge number of awards. It was recognized around the state as a major asset to the community and as having achieved excellence in journalism. Everyone understood what was expected of them, and everyone contributed.

The next year, however, things changed. Two of the six staff members left for other jobs. Their replacements, though, weren't nearly as committed to quality writing and reporting. The new people never realized their own missions, and were there simply to survive. As a result, the paper's effectiveness suffered. Important stories were never written, deadlines were missed, and the staff's morale plummeted. As an organization, the newspaper plunged to the ladder's lower rungs—survival mixed with periodic episodes of chaos.

If your goal is to achieve the highest rung on your ladder, ask yourself these three questions:

- How are you effective in your work or business, with your co-workers or business associates, your spouse and family, and in your social and other community interactions?
- What contributions have you made to your organization's goals?
- How can those contributions be enhanced?

Reaching the top rung of the ladder, while a reward in itself, isn't the end of the process. For just above the top rung of that ladder is the bottom rung of the next! And like any other worthwhile endeavor, this process of ladder climbing can be a challenge. But the potential rewards are great, with opportunities ahead that you could never have anticipated. Again, the ladder can serve as a simple reminder of the climbing process that accompanies any challenge you face. It can help you gauge where you are and where you need to go.

The next time you're thrust into or take on a new situation, consider the following and determine how you're going to approach the challenges that lies ahead:

- Are you approaching it with fear or excitement?
- How can you best survive the chaos?
- Have you already identified your mission and started charting the way to being the most effective you can be in your arena?

Again, there are ladders associated with everything—from work, to business ownership, to relationships, to education. The list is endless. Here's a series of questions you can answer to help you determine where you are now on your own ladder and help you focus on the most challenging area:

- Where are you on the ladder?
- What could motivate you to advance to the next rung?
- What specific steps can you take to get you there?
- What relationships do you need to establish to help with the process?
- How can you begin to restructure your use of your time to achieve this new goal?
- Who can you associate with and how can you best invest your time to achieve the next level?

You don't have to be the person officially designated as a *leader* to make positive contributions—no matter what the situation may be. There are tremendous opportunities to be effective at all levels. All it takes is your active involvement to bring it about.

Remember, if you don't choose to change, you've already reached your potential.

Chapter 21

When Failure Is Not an Option
What Would You Do If Success Were Assured?

*"Knowing how you're going
to accomplish your goal will allow you
to think in new, creative, and dynamic ways.
Having a structure in place will allow you to move forward
as you strive to achieve your dream."*
Michael Kerrigan

The threat of failure is something everyone, who is doing anything new or different, grapples with all the time, from closing a business deal to getting a response to a friendly smile.

The potential *not* to succeed is always around. And as a result, we may tend to limit our goals and dreams. We might think that if we don't aim too high, then the fallout from our failure won't be too painful.

But what if you were assured of success in whatever challenge you undertook? What if you could achieve anything you'd ever imagined—*anything?* On its face, attempting something without the threat of failure may seem like a pipe dream. We've all fantasized about meeting some challenge but, because of the possibility of failure or embarrassment, we've held ourselves back.

Now think about the last adventure you imagined yourself taking—but didn't. Did you allow the potential for failure to stand in your way? Did you concoct some other reason for not acting? Or was the choice beyond your control?

Are you concerned that experiencing a failure might indicate that you weren't equipped to succeed in the first place? Did you think you'd be ridiculed by others who just *knew* you couldn't pull it off?

Ironically, of course, these skeptics are generally passing judgment as they head out the door to a job they hate, or from the easy chair they rarely leave, or out of their *own* fear of failure.

So what would you attempt if you knew you could not fail? What great victory would you like to achieve?

Start thinking in a new way. Picture yourself pursuing your true wants with the assurance that you won't fail. Doing so will help you remove all the reasons for not taking positive steps in pursuit of your goal.

The "Insurance" Policy

Again, the attempt to claim something you've just been dreaming of may seem too good to even give it a shot. And that's why you're being supplied with a safety net, which first comes in the form of supportive *self-talk*—the encouragement you give yourself along the way to achieving your dream. How are you supporting yourself by what you say to yourself?

The safety net also comes in the form of support *networks*. These are the people with whom you associate in the process of achieving your goal. Who is supportive of you and smart enough to help you make the right choices?

Finally, the safety net is made up of supportive *systems*. These are the financial, religious, and other personal resources that provide you with various forms of "insurance" including: monetary, emotional, and a variety of new ideas you may have or learn about. What such components do you have in place that can help you achieve your success? Designing your support system—your safety net—is up to you. Fortunately each one of us has resources we can rely on right now. And with some thought, we can all determine the connections we need to make or nurture—with those who can help us achieve more success.

Knowing how you're going to accomplish your goal will allow you to think in new, creative, and dynamic ways. Having a structure in place will enable you to move forward as you strive to achieve your dream.

Gear up for some excitement. Attempting what you truly want will open up new opportunities and relationships that you may have never considered possible. Be prepared for the challenge *and* the success. You can handle it.

Chapter 22

Your Outcomes *Follow* Your Actions
Assume the Role of a Leader

*"Courage is simply the wisdom to
set a new course, and the ability and determination
to act in spite of your fear."*
Michael Kerrigan

Everyone wants to be in control, whether it's at work, in your business, at home, on the golf course with your eight iron, or someplace else. Masterful moves in a clear direction will give you a life that really means something—to both yourself and others.

This chapter contains many of the tools you can use to empower yourself, providing pathways to direct your life. And taking control is essential in establishing a new, permanent you.

Nothing but the Truth

The first element in taking control may appear to be simple but, for many, it's the most challenging step to take. The concept is so important, yet so basic, that the Sixth Commandment addresses it directly. While the commandment directs us not to lie, the more demanding task can be to *tell the truth.*

Of course, honesty is a simple concept. But many people find it nearly impossible to cope with honesty for a variety of reasons—the fear of consequences, the desire to avoid hurting other people's feelings, or the wish to gain some advantage. The reasons for not being honest are almost limitless—from political to financial, and from simple to complex.

Every one of us has a choice to make about how honest we're going to be every time we're asked a question. How you respond either comes out as the truth or something else—blurring, maneuvering, white lies, or maybe even excuses!

Whether the question is posed by another, or by *you*, how you respond will have immediate and lasting consequences. Being honest is the difference between a clear conscience and a firm direction, and something less—much less.

Consider Jason and *the agreement*. In June 1996 Jason signed a contract with a friend from his days as an engineer in Atlanta. The old friend would act as an agent for Jason, who had developed a revolutionary line of sparkplugs. But rather than a simple statement of what his friend would do for Jason and how he'd be paid, the agreement stretched over four pages, littered with a confounding jumble of wherefores and shalls.

What Jason envisioned as a simple working document turned into a complex web of legalisms that called for him to surrender a significant percentage of profits, an interest in the patent, and locked him into the deal for three years. Only after a month of haggling and revamping did Jason finally agree.

Reaching an agreement was only the first step in a square dance of disappointments. One surprise followed another. What Jason thought would be a creative, well-connected team working on his behalf turned out to be anything but. The venture was plagued by false starts, overpromises, and flagging commitment. And Jason regretted the relationship.

But rather than question his partner's approach, Jason deferred. He put off saying anything for the next three months. Rather than being open and honest, he was something else. Jason didn't want to interfere with an approach that might actually pay off in his sparkplugs going national. He also didn't want to hurt his old friend's feelings. So he waited.

The end of the relationship came without much warning. Jason's friend called one day to say he didn't have much feel for what step to take next. So what did Jason think? It was obvious that the relationship was useless. The marketing that was supposed to be provided by the old friend wasn't real.

At that point, Jason finally found the courage to be honest and he terminated the agreement. The moment he made that decision, he was flooded with his own ideas about how to market the plugs, identify financing, and create new products. Honesty relieved Jason of the pressure of worrying, and freed him to make the best choices he could for himself—so he could realize his goals. Yes, honesty is the best policy!

Whatever You Say

The next element of taking control of your life is mastering those conversations you have with yourself—*controlling your scripts*. Unfortunately, these thoughts and messages are often contaminated. Rather than an aid to living an effective life, your scripts can become a burden—or worse.

Consider Katherine. Her skill as a graphic artist was admired by just about everyone who saw her work. Her drawing ability led to a full-time position on the art staff of a regional magazine. She had a lot of insight and was sought out by coworkers for the humor behind her easy grin.

But the scripts that haunted Katherine were negative and destructive. And that internal dialogue surfaced as cutting remarks that she directed at herself. She criticized her own body shape as short and wide, and attacked the silly grin that most of her friends found so endearing.

Katherine panicked when deadlines approached. She told herself that her flawless drawings didn't measure up to the magazine's standards and would probably be rejected—although they never were. In fact, her work was usually the object of great praise.

Finally, she took a leave from the magazine simply to get away and never returned. She had left behind a promising career in a supportive environment, and it was all her negative internal scripts which were undermining and untrue.

Now let's take a look at the quality of one of your own scripts. While they probably aren't nearly as destructive as Katherine's were, consider any examples of ineffective dialogue you might be using on yourself:

- What kind of instructions are you giving yourself that aren't getting you what you need? What's keeping you from being successful in a certain area of your life?

- If you can't recall something you've been telling yourself in the past, think of some negative messages you're passing on to someone else—your spouse, your kids, a coworker, a business associate, or an employee.
- Would it be better to completely abandon this script, or does the message need to be communicated in some other way?
- If it does need to be communicated differently, how could you rephrase it to get a better result?

It's Coming to Me

Before your scripts can gel into words, whether they are of inspiration or terror, they have to present themselves as mental messages. And some of the most instructive thoughts we can have are the *idle* ones. The guidance here is simple—*pay attention to your idle thoughts.*

They flash in your mind, wedged between focused concentration and deep sleep. But all too often these blips of information are dismissed as so much static. They're swept aside like advertising until the *real* show inside your brain resumes.

But idle thoughts *are* part of the real show. They are fragments of ideas, plans, or directions bidding for your attention. And listening to them can open up a whole new world of possibilities for you.

The next time an idle thought wanders across your brain, write it down in your planner or on a blank sheet of paper. It may have to do with money, a vacation, a relationship, or your dream house—or all four. Just be sure to write it down.

Notice the next idle thought that interrupts your regular thought pattern. Write that down as well, and so on throughout the day. Start with a time block of eight hours or so. If this isn't enough time, then extend it.

You may fill up the page, or you may have only one or two entries, depending on how much information is out there trying to make an impression on you. At the end of the day, review the list. What have you written down that you'd expect to see? What entry is a complete surprise, or even a shock? Now, how are you going to address these issues?

Think of this process as something like your e-mail. Can you glance at the heading and delete it without any thought? Do you ask yourself if the message is something you need to open and pay attention to? Or is it something you need to act on *now*?

If you delete an idea and it keeps coming back, there may be something to it that you are unwilling to recognize or admit. There's more to living than just doing the task at hand. Being aware of idle thoughts and paying attention to them will help increase your awareness and control over the things that are truly important.

I Was Just Thinking

The next step in taking control is a mental exercise where you can—*use your creative imagination.*

When I was growing up, my friend Gregg was reluctant to go where he hadn't been before. He would typically respond with the phrase "I just can't picture that" when he was faced with some new challenge.

The range of what he couldn't imagine was vast. He couldn't picture climbing the flatirons—the large stone pillars that jutted out of the mountains above town. He couldn't imagine going to college anywhere except right there at home. He couldn't envision asking the most attractive girl in school to the junior-senior prom.

And in the end, he never ventured past the boulder field that lay just below the flatirons. He attended the university two miles away. And Gregg and that most beautiful girl—who, not so incidentally, was interested in him—never said anything more than *hello* when they passed in the halls. They certainly never went to the prom together. What Gregg couldn't imagine, he never did.

Now think of any successful athlete who ever competed on the field, or any performer or speaker who ever took the stage. In every case you'll find that before they ever changed into a uniform or applied the makeup or attached the microphone to their clothing, they pictured themselves performing in that role. Not only did they perform, they succeeded in every way imaginable, fulfilling their own expectations and earning the applause and cheers of the crowd.

Once you begin to mentally see yourself triumphantly doing, engaging, or performing in any setting, the mystery is removed. It is replaced by the possibility. And when you acknowledge the possibility of success, taking the steps to succeed, becomes normal, logical, and desirable. It's a natural progression. *In your mind you've created a new comfort zone.*

Gregg never saw the possibility. In his mind, there was nothing to evolve toward. The challenge always seemed too great. At least he *thought* it was.

In this exercise, think of one instance in which you've used your creative imagination to begin the process of achieving what you had only been dreaming of before.

- First, what was the circumstance in which you imagined yourself succeeding before you ever acted?
- Second, what was the actual outcome?
- Was the outcome the one you had envisioned?
- If it wasn't, what interfered with your getting the best result?
- Now think of three upcoming situations in which you might use your creative imagination to bring about the best possible result. These might include speaking before a group, meeting with a new prospect or client, or asking someone new for a date.

Whatever the task is, if you are not preparing in advance for the outcome you want, start getting ready now. Before you accept a challenge, picture yourself succeeding at it.

Keep on Going

The next step to taking personal control deals with staying focused—*learn to persist.*

Persistence is more than continuing a game of phone tag until you finally have a conversation. Sure, that may be a part of it. But persistence really means pursuing your goal by *doing whatever it takes*—until it's fully achieved!

We all learn to persist early in life. When we're in school, or training for some profession or degree, persistence is normal. But once we leave the environment that says *you will*, our persistence may leave too. Our will to accomplish the task, which needs to be focused, is more likely to be pulled in a hundred different directions by everything from kids to television, travel to sleep.

Consider the last time you persisted and finally achieved what you wanted. Recalling the event—and remembering the steps you took to achieve it—will help reinforce your success and give you a model for pursuing your current goal.

Test Yourself

Next—*learn from your mistakes.*

While you may think that mistakes are acts that should be avoided at all costs—or put behind you as quickly as possible—they can be some of the best teachers you'll ever have. In fact, you'll learn more from adverse circumstances than you will from textbook successes—as long as you pay attention to what the mistake is telling you.

Mistakes come in a variety of forms and a range of predicaments. Every one of us has our own examples from experiences where we misjudged or misspoke, where we acted when we could have better stood still, or ignored some event that turned into a disaster. Look back on just one of those episodes from your life and think about how that event affects the way you act now.

On the other hand, purposely *not* making mistakes can be just as instructive, when you take an honest look at your motivation. The problem is, this can be just a maneuver to maintain status quo—to not risk failing.

I recently went skiing with some friends who brought along their young son, Robbie. Now even though Robbie has been on skis only half a dozen times or so, he's developed some skills and can navigate most of the slopes he encounters. After our trip, Robbie reported that he didn't even fall once. He hadn't embarrassed himself or suffered any discomfort by making a mistake. He considered all that a great accomplishment.

But by not pushing himself—by playing it safe—Robbie didn't improve, either. By not risking making a mistake, he hadn't learned anything new. He stayed precisely where he was.

Opportunities to risk making mistakes are everywhere. The challenge is to see the benefit when you stumble and make one.

I *Do* Believe in Ghosts

Finally—*harness your courage.*

Setting a new course for your life isn't for the fainthearted. Nobody goes through life unafraid. At one time or another, each of us has had a twinge of doubt about a bold new move. And that's why you need to summon your nerve.

Courage is simply the wisdom to set a new course, and the ability and determination to *act in spite of* your fear. When you're charting a course for a new way of conducting yourself, you're going to encounter new demands. And while this creates an opportunity for fear to creep in, keep in mind that no courage is required where there is no fear. If you're not experiencing any fear, you're probably not growing!

To forestall fear or overcome its effects, you need to examine the process you're getting involved in. Break it down into as many steps as you need to make you feel comfortable with it. As Helen Keller once said, "The world is moved not only by the mighty shoves of the heroes but also by the aggregate of the tiny pushes of each honest worker."

No doubt you can remember outlining a report for your high school English class. The assignment of a 10-page typed report may have seemed daunting, if not impossible, when it was first made. But as you thought about it, you began to break the task down into its parts. First came the topic, which was then followed by major categories: A, B, C, and D, or more if the issue was more complex. You then broke down each one of those categories into subcategories 1, 2, and 3, and every one had specific points of discussion of their own.

As you addressed each small part of the challenge and resolved it, you progressed toward achieving your goal. And the project that may have seemed impossible when it was first assigned became manageable—the whole was nothing more than the sum of all its little parts.

As you move forward in creating a new life, manage it simply by managing the small parts. These are the building blocks of success to give yourself an outcome you'll embrace every day. As a bonus, you'll also be a great example and role model for others.

Chapter 23

It's About Time for a Change
Schedule Your Steps to Success

*"Concentrate on what part of your life
you want to change, when you plan to do it, and the
exact steps you're going to take to achieve it."*
Michael Kerrigan

A whole industry has grown up around the subject of time. Day Timers, Franklin Planners, Palm Pilots, and appointment calendars all detail—with accountant-like precision—when and where and with whom you'll meet.

With the introduction of these tools, getting to and from appointments with split-second timing has progressed from an art to a science. Such scheduling documents, like evidence rendered at a trial, give proof to people's growing, almost reflexive response of "I don't have time." Any deviation from the schedule in the book is something akin to a sin.

"I don't have time." How many times have you heard it this week, or even today? How many times have you said it yourself, and verified it with your leather-bound appointment book? "Just look at this," you say to an associate, flashing day after day of crowded pages of appointments, "I don't have time for anything!"

While the day planner may keep you on track for your appointments, there is one important thing it can't do. It can't tell you if you are doing the *right* things.

Ask yourself if your appointment book is useful to you in better affording you the opportunity to change and grow. Or is it just helping you lock yourself into a tighter and more controlled routine?

This is where *desire* comes in to play. You can always make the time—when you truly want to. There is a larger choice here, just waiting for you to make it, and doing that will help determine where you go with the rest of your life.

There's no doubt you have a demanding schedule. And if you're married, you have a spouse and perhaps children who require your time and attention. On top of your family is your job or business, which may be demanding *only* eight hours a day, but is probably taking much more. Then there is eating, sleeping, showering, traveling, and catching your breath.

When you factor in all of these commitments, doing whatever needs to be done, the day may be over. You might think there isn't time for anything new. But there's always time to redirect your life—*when you decide that it's a priority.*

Charting Your Change

Next, let's create a timeline that—from beginning to end—represents 24 hours. This is your 24-hour timeline on an average day.

Get a pen and block out periods of time on this line. First, mark off eight hours for sleep, or whatever amount of time you require. Then figure eight hours, or more, for work, and then add in commuting time.

Next, estimate the amount of time you need for running errands, taking children to their activities, and visiting with family and friends, and enter that on the line. If you exercise, figure that in next. Then enter the time you need for meals. If you're average, 21 of your 24 hours have been accounted for.

Next, give yourself an hour or so for downtime. This is for staring out the window, daydreaming, and going to the restroom. Then there is television and computer time, which may overlap with the zone-out time you just entered.

With these additional activities, your 24 hours are probably used up. But even if they're not, you're undoubtedly close to having all of your available time accounted for. And you're likely to be asking yourself, "Where do I fit in a new life? Where do I even begin to think about change?"

Look again at the timeline. Even if the time *not* claimed by your other activities amounts to only five or ten minutes, start there to introduce change into your routine. If you have the luxury of a free hour, the answer is easy.

If every available minute on the timeline is claimed by something, look closely at what you're doing. What activity can be trimmed back to allow you to do something new?

Can the two hours you may spend zoned-out or propped in front of the television or surfing the Internet each night be cut back to one, or eliminated altogether? Imagine using that time to make some dreams come true, perhaps by building a business on the side.

If you walk before or after work, or even at coffee breaks or lunch, start to outline how you're going to change during your walks. (Remember to take along a note pad or recorder to capture your *idle thoughts*.) Concentrate on what part of your life you want to change, when you plan to do it, and the exact steps you're going to take to achieve it.

Look at the other entries on your timeline and how they might be accomplished faster, more efficiently, or delegated to someone else. Whether you control only 0.2 percent or 20 percent of the timeline, begin your change there.

Of course, if you're determined to resist change, you can always find an excuse. But since you're committed to greater success in your life, look in your day planner, pick a page, and tell yourself, "I'm making the time to make my dream of _____ come true, starting today!"

Chapter 24

Decide to Commit to Change
Clarify Who You Are and Where You're Going

*"Taking deliberate action to influence your outcomes and achieve
what you want presents a more challenging path. Those who take it
are the exception. They're the ones who succeed—the only ones."*
Michael Kerrigan

When it comes to establishing a new goal and changing a
behavior so you can reach it, you may be saying, "I understand it in theory, but I'm not ready to commit to it."
Reaching this point is normal—with relationships, jobs, businesses,
political action, and dozens of other areas in people's lives.

Just about anyone can master concepts. But taking deliberate action to influence your outcomes and achieve what you want presents
a more challenging path. Those who take it are the exception.
They're the ones who succeed—the *only* ones.

Unless you commit to reach your goals and persist as you carry
out your plan of action, life can be a hollow, boring exercise. If
you're not accustomed to making and keeping promises, committing can be as alien as walking on the moon. If you've made a
resolution and kept it before, you know the process is as simple—
and as challenging—as doing what you say you will do. Success
comes in the follow through.

Committing is the conscious act of saying, "This is who I
choose to be and what I choose to do." See it through until you
complete it, then set an even bigger goal to pursue. *Acting* on
your own behalf with the best information you have needs to be
your priority.

You already know life comes with no guarantees. But focusing and executing your plan can help you make every step you take a positive one toward your goals. Change is a process, and striving to create the life you want is a sign of strength.

Now think of one thing, person, or cause you're committed to. It can involve a pledge to do something, or to bind yourself emotionally or intellectually to someone or some course of action.

Without commitment, life can be fleeting, taking you from one person, one place of worship, or one job or business to the next—with no sense of fulfillment or reward along the way. Remember the trauma Phil went through as he attained various degrees and held assorted jobs—and still came up empty?

Making a commitment gives a sense of meaning, accomplishment, and peace. Once made, each step you take will have a greater impact and meaning. Committing helps you focus on something that's important to you, helps you clarify your thinking, and guides your actions. It enables you to let go of behaviors that are getting in your way.

When you've given the issue or opportunity some thought and are ready to take a stand or get started, declaring your commitment won't be a problem. If you haven't thought about it, begin now. Your commitment may be to improving a personal relationship, creating a new business, developing a more effective behavior, or helping a respected cause.

If you're having trouble committing to a dream, a new way of behaving, or any other worthwhile endeavor, you may not have clarified your roles and responsibilities to yourself. Unless you have a clear sense of who you are and where you are going, charting a course for the rest of your life can be an overwhelming challenge. But it's so worthwhile doing.

If you need assistance in making a solid commitment, take some time to answer the following four questions. Your answers will help you identify who you are, what's truly important to you, and what you're most capable of achieving.

The first question is: "Who am I?" This is more than looking up your name in the telephone book. It demands more of you than calling your parents or friends and asking them to explain how they define you.

- Are you the person who never misses a meeting, or has the best-manicured lawn on the block?
- Are you the one who teaches your children to play fairly and with concern for others?
- Are you secretly composing a symphony in the basement?
- Or are you a blend of all of these qualities, or something else?

Next, ask yourself: "What are my expectations of me?" We all have various self-expectations. They come in the form of jobs, businesses or challenges—like climbing mountains, registering top sales, or doing something else extraordinary. The key to pursuing and achieving these expectations is to *focus.*

- Are you fulfilling your wants and needs?
- Are you pursuing an established goal?
- Or are you taking your life's cues from those around you, without any real sense of direction or mission?

The third question is: "What are my responsibilities?" Defining your responsibilities will help you clarify the strengths you already have, and point out areas of your life you may never have explored.

- What do you absolutely need to do?
- What obligations do you have because of a spoken promise or written document?
- Are those responsibilities detailed, for example, in the agreement you signed to build a house, or your obligation to raise your children to be educated, responsible adults who contribute to society?

Finally, ask yourself: "Where are my connections?" They're your link to relationships, and help you establish your place in society.

- Who or what are you connected to?
- Do your loyalties extend to a group of friends from college, to your coworkers, your employer's company, your own business, or to those leaders who have helped you get where you are?
- What about respect and love for yourself and others?

Answer these four questions and you'll probably have a good sense of who you are and your ability to commit. Unfortunately, for some, the search for identity is never achieved. They wander through life on the verge of discovering who they truly are and what they really want, but they don't go the extra mile to find out.

If you can answer these questions, yet think there's a better way to live, it may be time for a change. Journey down a road that allows you to accept life's challenges and craft your own solutions—while knowing exactly who you are and where you are going.

Chapter 25

Reach for Your Goal
Establish Long-Lasting Change

*"By its very nature, goal setting
imposes new ways of behaving. It introduces change.
And each step you take toward your new goal and a brighter future
takes you a step further from the way things were."*
Michael Kerrigan

When was the last time you set goals? Did you sit down to do some serious planning on New Year's Day or your birthday? Or were the circumstances more crisis-driven—in the wake of a professional or personal challenge?

How long did you pursue your goals—a day, a week, a month, or more than a year? And where did your new goals get you?

Many people waste time setting goals because they then fail to pursue them. They aren't really wholeheartedly commited to achieving them. And, all too often, they don't give them any priority, making them easy to dismiss.

Goal setting is the most important element in initiating and managing meaningful, effective, long-lasting change. Short-term goals can help you get to work on time, spend more time with your kids or spouse, or mow the lawn. And these short or transitional efforts have their own rewards. But achieving *long-term* goals will have a significant impact on the way you live the rest of your life. This level of goal setting requires a focused effort. And while this isn't a 12-step program in the popular sense, here are 12 steps to help you reach your long-term goals.

Step 1—*Choose Your Goal*

Be as specific as you can be. People deal in generalities every day, but where does that get them? Your goal may be to have a better life, and that's fine. But how do you want your life to improve—*specifically?* Does it involve your finances, your job or your business, your relationships, or your recognition in the community?

Give your goal a name and a face. Make it just as clear and identifiable as your image in the mirror. It's only when you make your goal specific that you can take meaningful steps to achieve it.

I'm reminded of Nick. Born in New York City, he moved to San Francisco after working for years in the Arizona copper mines. His life was loaded with experiences others could only imagine.

Nick's goal was to be a writer. And he became one. He ended up as a senior writer for an environmental group. But what he *really* wanted to be was a novelist.

Be as specific as you can in identifying your goal. Sometimes being just *a writer* isn't enough.

Step 2—*Identify the Benefits of Reaching Your Goal*

Do the benefits include doing what you enjoy, money (perhaps financial freedom), position, or prestige? And for *whom* are you setting this goal? Too often, goals are set just to inappropriately please other people, from family and friends to neighbors and business associates. But who benefits from a goal set just to please somebody else? It may be that the person or people you may be trying to please, when it comes right down to it, might not care particularly *what* you do. You may just *think* it pleases them!

You are the one who needs to handle any consequences and hopefully gets to enjoy the benefits of achieving your goal. So you need to want it for yourself. Otherwise, you're setting yourself up to create a situation you may not want—which could be quite a disappointing outcome.

The one thing Brad wanted more than anything in the world was to escape his occupation of putting together complicated real estate deals. He was weary of it because it had become drudgery for him. He was ready to change direction, and finally realized that it was his choice whether or not to move on. He didn't have to remain stuck doing something he really didn't enjoy.

Brad's dream was to lead adventure trips. Whether it was on skis, backpacking above 14,000 feet, or whitewater rafting, his goal was to be challenged by the outdoors. The challenge with this goal was that it didn't pay nearly enough for Brad's needs. The financial benefits in reaching his goal of adventure just didn't measure up. So he stayed in his job selling commercial real estate. And he convinced himself into believing that leading outdoor excursions wasn't realistic.

Brad could have decided to do what he loved to do outdoors as a part-time venture. He could have experimented with various aspects of it until he found out more specifically what he liked the most and how he could live his dream. It may have included building a business after hours where he could, in association with others, set himself up financially so he could lead adventure trips whenever he wanted to. But Brad gave up and did what nearly 70 percent of people do—settle for a life they aren't happy with, thinking they have no choice.

Step 3—*Picture Yourself With Your Goal Met*

Successful people use their creative imaginations every day. They see themselves making a sale, taking a stand, correcting a wrong, building a business or career, or even running a country.

Let your mind achieve your goal before you start going for it. You'll save yourself the time, money, and the stress of chasing a goal that may prove to be something you don't want because of all the circumstances that accompany it. Do your homework.

Suppose your goal is to be an acclaimed war correspondent. That's great. But picture yourself operating under the following conditions: You're forced to spend weeks, if not months, away from your family and friends. You're exposed to random, hazardous situations that could get you killed. You're filing provocative stories under deadline pressure, while dodging government censors who may or may not let you report your story.

Of course, you could win the Pulitzer Prize. Or you could go crazy from frustration. Just be sure to picture all the possibilities and what they'd be like before you commit to your goal. Know that what you are setting out to do is to achieve something you honestly desire.

Step 4—*List the Obstacles You Need to Overcome in Reaching Your Goal*

If your goal is to be a champion skier, and you've never been on a pair of skis, your first obstacle is obvious—learning to ski. Liking the sport is an important next step, while becoming proficient enough to race and win are three more levels of challenges you'll need to overcome.

Just be aware that, whatever your goal is, there will be obstacles. Fortunately, in most cases, they'll be less ominous than those for the totally inexperienced would-be ski racer who, living in balmy weather, goes north and discovers he or she doesn't even like snow!

Step 5—*Identify Groups and Individuals You Can Work With to Achieve Your Goal*

In politics, they're called constituents—a group of people, from diverse backgrounds, with a common interest in seeing one candidate elected or a ballot issue passed. In business, such people may be called associates or affiliates who form networks of independent business owners.

The concept of building coalitions can have a direct and beneficial impact on achieving your goal. It's far easier to work with others in a common effort than it is to rely solely on yourself.

Of course, support doesn't come without a cost. Constituents typically want some kind of return for their time, or money, or knowledge—usually in the form of a vote, or a bill, or an appointment. Businesspeople expect to reap financial benefits in exchange for their time and energy. (In a new business startup, this can take a while to realize, so people generally do it on the side first.)

In the best possible case, you're creating positive outcomes where everyone involved in your effort will benefit. Just remember that you don't have to go it alone. Take advantage of the chance to join with others in a cooperative effort.

Step 6—*List the Skills and Knowledge You'll Need to Reach Your Goal*

If your goal is to be a motivational speaker, you'll need to develop an area of expertise, train your voice, perhaps do it free at first, and plug into a lecture circuit. Loving to talk and be around people is a given.

If your goal is to be a trial attorney, you'll have to get through law school, pass the bar exam, invest some time on the staff of the district attorney or public defender, and learn to sway a jury.

If your goal is to be an independent business owner, you'll need to find leaders in your industry who are where you want to be. Learn from them, follow their recommendations for success, and plug into a continuing education program. There's always a process involved in reaching each and every goal, and acquiring the skills and knowledge you'll need plays a big part.

I'm reminded of a woman who graduated from the University of Denver. She wanted to move on from her role as a housewife and become a communications specialist. After enrolling in the program at the age of 70, she received her Ph.D. at the age of 76, and began her consulting practice. She identified and acquired the skills required to reach her goal, and she convinced herself that it wasn't too late to reach the goal she truly wanted. In other words, she made no excuses!

Step 7—*Set a Target Date for Reaching Your Goal*

Anybody who wants to achieve anything will respond to a deadline. Some people are more measured in their pace, as they work methodically toward the deadline, getting a little work done each day until the task is completed. Others put off doing anything until the deadline is looming, and then they scramble to start and finish their work. In most cases, deadlines are met, whether it's out of desire, necessity, or panic. Reaching your goal will probably be similar. The process may not always be pretty— marred by fits and starts—but at least you'll get there as long as you stay focused on your goal and persevere.

Now when Ted was without a deadline, he never produced. It was as if work assignments didn't even exist. The work could always be done tomorrow, or later than that, he thought.

Unless he was close to a deadline and threatened by the boss breathing down his neck if he missed it, work assignments were nothing more than stacks of paper cluttering his desk. But when Ted was given a target date, he met it. The process he followed wasn't always neat and tidy, but, nonetheless, the quality of his work was exceptional. And that's all his boss cared about.

Regardless of how you work, target dates will help keep you focused on achieving your identified goal.

Step 8—*Write Down Your Plan of Action*

Again, be as specific as you can in detailing your plan. Jumping from where you are now—point A—to where you finally want to be—point Z—can be pretty intimidating if you don't know the steps you'll be taking in between. And, under these circumstances, ambiguity can be one of your most aggressive enemies. If you haven't identified the specific actions you're going to take, vagueness can take over, like it does for most people, and cause you to drift aimlessly.

When you start to focus on the specific steps—B through Y—reaching your goal becomes easier. Write down daily, weekly, and monthly plans that will move you closer to your goal.

Let's say you're writing a book. Set targets for finishing your research, organizing your material, writing an outline, completing your first draft, making revisions, and submitting the completed package to your publisher.

At every step along the way, evaluate where you are in reaching your goal and make adjustments as necessary to get or keep yourself on course. Use the next three steps as reinforcing tools:

Step 9—*Reward Yourself for Your Progress Along the Way*

It's a mistake to think that you're going to achieve any major goal with little effort and a minimum of inconvenience. Look at reaching it as a worthwhile, long-term endeavor.

To get where you are going, you will need to reach smaller intermediate goals—in the process of reaching your main goal. Recognize these events as mileposts. They might include printing your first marketing brochure, landing your first client or associate, or receiving your first paycheck or bonus check.

Always encourage yourself with rewards to continue achieving these incremental victories. Remember that a relationship isn't a success only if it reaches a 25th anniversary. It needs to be a success every day. A hug or a kiss, a kind word or a loving note or card given at random will be much appreciated by your spouse and you'll feel good about doing it.

No matter what your goal or dream is, make the journey rewarding. It'll help you keep yourself focused on reaching your major goal. And always remember to enjoy the trip. After all, each day needs to be enjoyed as you move on.

Step 10—*Remind Yourself Daily of What Your Goal Is and Structure Your Time Around Achieving It*

Remind yourself of your goal to stay on track. Write it down and post it where you'll see it daily—on a wall, mirror, refrigerator, or wherever it can serve you as a consistently seen catalyst for you to take action. *In sight, in mind.* This daily reminder can help you funnel your energies into achieving what you want, rather than allowing daily distractions to deter you.

Participating in support activities is important because they help keep you focused. This can include books and periodicals, educational/motivational video tapes or CDs, continuing education audio tapes, seminars, conventions and other growth opportunities, people you spend your time with—even the nature of your conversations.

In assessing how you're spending your time, look at how you've structured your average day. Are you able to devote enough time to achieve your goal, or are you just kidding yourself? Are you investing your time or just wiling it away? Reaching your goal may require little more than adjusting blocks of time here and there. It may demand that you restructure how you're spending large portions of your day. You may discover that the efforts to reach your goal will be all encompassing, especially in the beginning.

How you structure your time is directly related to your dedication to your goal and how soon you want to reach it. How serious are you about achieving it?

Step 11—*Remember to Affirm Your Goal Frequently*

Saying, "This is what I want" doesn't make you selfish or obsessed. It is a statement of truth. Asserting yourself will keep you focused on your goal. Encouragement, both in your self-talk and from others, will help keep you passionate about the prospect of achieving what you want. So be positive and associate with people who care enough about you to root you on.

Reminding yourself of your goal doesn't have to become an endless recording, repeated dozens of times every minute—that approaches drudgery and persuasion. Since you've made it this far, you already believe in the merit of what you're doing and aiming toward. Cheering yourself on, telling yourself "I can do it," serves as a reminder of where you're headed and why.

Step 12—*Watch Out for Old Habits Trying to Sneak Their Way Back Into Your Life*

Goal setting's very nature imposes new ways of behaving—it introduces change. And every step you take toward your new goals and brighter future takes you one step further from the way things *were*.

Under changing circumstances, some people panic. They freeze out of fear, or out of the uneasiness that comes from uncertainty or a sense of loss. The easiest way to react to these perfectly normal, predictable feelings is to return to the old way. However, that's taking the path of regret. And *guaranteed*, in 100 percent of the cases, acting in the old way is *never* the way to a new goal.

A friend of mine used to say that the easiest way to get over the tension from quitting smoking would be to have a cigarette. His goal was to quit, but his old ways told him he needs a pack a day to do it. He was looking for a rationale to smoke instead of a reason strong enough to overcome his old reaction to stress—smoking.

Be careful of being seduced by your old habits. They can lure you into the trap of staying stuck—and not accomplishing whatever your goal is—which robs you of the benefits you could be experiencing. They cloud your vision and cause your focus to blur. Old habits coax you into the very behaviors you may be endeavoring to overcome. They relieve you of the necessary conscious control and clarity you need to reach your goals.

Chapter 26

Direct Your Efforts to Get Results
Touch Base With Reality

*"Make sure the steps you're taking toward
your goal are positive mentally, physically, and socially.
Satisfy yourself that you're happier now than you were before you
started down this road to change."*
Michael Kerrigan

Virtually everyone wrestles with themselves, to one degree or another, over what to do with their lives. This mentally going back and forth is usually pretty harmless stuff, though, consisting of self-doubt, second-guessing, and perhaps gorging on snack food.

Of course, not everyone wants to let him or herself off so easily. Their internal conflict sometimes escalates to the next step. Some people meet themselves in a mental boxing ring and aren't happy until they've beaten themselves up so badly that they abandon their efforts to achieve new goals. And change becomes an exercise they will never attempt again.

When you want to redirect your life, subjecting yourself to physical and mental mayhem is definitely *not* the way to go—it's not even close to what you need to be doing. There is a way to get productive feedback about the change you're making, and not have to suffer a bloody nose in the process.

Checking your direction consists of four questions you can ask yourself at any time once you decide to change the way you're operating.

Is This a Positive Direction for Me?

Make sure the steps you're taking toward your goal are positive—mentally, physically, and socially. Satisfy yourself that you're happier now than you were before you started down this road to change. If you aren't sure you're on the right path, reevaluate what you want and what steps you need to take to get there. Ask for help from an expert, if that's needed.

Do I Respect Myself Now More Than I Did Before?

If you *don't* hold yourself in higher personal regard than you did before you started your change, stop. Ask yourself why this is true, make the necessary changes, and keep moving. Just continuing to do what you're doing is likely to end in failure and put you back in the boxing ring for another defeat.

We all need respect, and self-respect is the most important. That's where it all starts. How we regard ourselves reflects itself in all we think, say, and do. How can you truly respect yourself?

Am I Taking Care of My Needs?

Ignoring your basic needs by making huge, painful sacrifices in the name of change is a fundamental mistake. If you don't take care of yourself, you won't be of much good to others. Effective, meaningful change brings with it a sense of peace and satisfaction.

Be sure to pay attention to all aspects of your life when you're changing a behavior or establishing a goal.

Am I Achieving What I Set Out to Do?

If you've implemented a change and the results aren't what you wanted or expected, rethink what you're doing.

If you're harming people in this process, and perhaps doing something illegal, immoral, or unethical, then you need to change your approach. Some people's behavior is obnoxious and offensive, without them even realizing it. If you would ever do that, you'd alienate rather than befriend people. Observe your behavior and how people react to you. Would you like to be treated like that? Is your behavior something you'll need to rethink to accomplish your goal?

If your new way is helping you achieve what you want—without violating the first three points—keep it up. You're on the right track.

Conclusion

"You'll notice a difference—a positive difference—in the way you live each day and the way change finally plays out in the months and years to come."
Michael Kerrigan

Change is inevitable. But dealing with it successfully isn't. There's nothing automatic about living life to its fullest. You need to become involved. And the payoff is a better understanding of yourself, fuller relationships with others, and greater rewards in every opportunity that arises.

Yet too many people continue to turn their backs on the challenges change brings, or they walk away from the opportunity to influence the outcomes that change creates. As you've already read, life doesn't have to be that way.

Of course, not every business interaction will seem to go your way. Not every person will do precisely what you want him or her to do. But exerting yourself to go beyond the limits you may have placed on yourself, whenever you have the opportunity, will make a difference. You'll notice a difference—a positive difference—in the way you live each day and the way change finally plays out in the months and years to come.

Redirecting your life means first taking total responsibility for it. While charting your actions and outcomes may seem pretty demanding, it's the most liberating thing you can do. To establish yourself as the chief player in your life will lay the foundation for positive and productive outcomes. Anything less leaves someone else in control, which usually leads to frustration and unhappiness.

You *can* influence your outcomes—whatever your dreams and goals may be. Making it happen hinges directly on establishing what you want and guiding your actions to achieve that end, whatever it takes. You *can* become the architect for designing who you become and where you go from this day forward.

What choice do you have? Whatever it is that you want!

And remember, as the philosopher Albert Camus once said...

"Life is the sum of all your choices."

About the Author

Michael Kerrigan is a motivational speaker, mediator, and president of Lifetracks Unlimited, a company that creates lifeskills programs and training materials for adults and young people.

He worked as an investigative reporter and national correspondent, having spent more than a decade with newspapers and magazines around the U.S.

Michael recently finished work on a children's book on negotiating, and has produced four series of audiotape programs focusing on change, choice making, reaching one's potential, and relationship building. He lives in Colorado and you can contact him via e-mail at Michael@SeventhRail.com or his website at www.SeventhRail.com.

"The strongest
principle of
growth lies in
human choice."

—George Elliot